EFFECTIVE EVANGELISM

The Divine Art of Soul-Winning

J Oswald Sanders was born and educated in New Zealand, where he still lives. For many years he was principal of the Christian Leaders' Training College in New Guinea. He is now a consulting director for Overseas Missionary Fellowship, and travels widely to meet a heavy schedule of Christian conference and other speaking engagements. His many books include *Spiritual Leadership, Spiritual Maturity, People Just Like Us, Satan No Myth, Enjoying Growing Old, Prayer Power Unlimited* and *The Incomparable Christ.*

EFFECTIVE EVANGELISM

The Divine Art of Soul-Winning

J Oswald Sanders

STL BOOKS

P O Box 48, Bromley, Kent, England
P O Box 28, Waynesboro, Georgia, USA
P O Box 656, Bombay 13, India

© 1982 J Oswald Sanders
A revised edition of *The Divine Art of Soul-Winning*.

STL Books are published by Send The Light
(Operation Mobilisation), 9 London Road,
Bromley, Kent, England.

ISBN 0 903843 58 7

Cover photograph by courtesy of the British
Tourist Authority.

Made and Printed in Great Britain by
Hunt Barnard Printing Ltd, Aylesbury, Bucks.

Contents

Preface to Revised Edition

It is almost fifty years since the first edition of this book was published under the title *The Divine Art of Soul-Winning*. It owed its origin to a series of lectures I delivered to students of the Bible College of New Zealand on the subject of personal evangelism. Some of the material is dated, and I have rewritten the book. The passing of the years has changed my views on many subjects, but not on the value of a human soul, and the importance of individual witness in evangelism. Indeed in an age when mass production and mass movements are the order of the day, the importance of the individual should receive even more emphasis.

Mass evangelism, radio evangelism, pastoral evangelism all have their place; but the most effective method is still that of motivating concerned Christians to present the claims of Christ personally to those who are still in the kingdom of darkness.

The former title of the book indicated that winning people to Christ is an art to be learned from the Master fisher of men. It was Jesus who used this figure when He said to Peter and Andrew, 'Follow me, and I will make you fishers of men' – and all fishermen know that theirs is a fine art that must be learned.

However, learning to lead people to faith in Christ is not merely a matter of mastering methods and techniques. There is no such thing as 'Ten Easy Lessons in Soul-Winning'. That can be a mere intellectual exercise with no personal involvement. The effective personal evangelist is motivated by love and loyalty to the Lord who came 'to seek and to save those who were lost'. He is moved by the fact that those without Christ are under the judgment of God. He is gripped by the fact that he has been entrusted with a message that can change their destiny from hell to heaven, and bring untold blessing into their lives and homes.

Having personally witnessed people in missionary situations becoming Christians the very first time they heard the gospel message, I have unbounded confidence in the power of the Word of God to bring light and life to darkened souls anywhere in the world.

In the church of which I am currently a member, there have been many conversions during the past year, and the majority of them are the result of home visitation and personal evangelism. A revival of this form of Christian service is one of the surest ways to bring renewal to the church. I preached recently in an American church. Among those who responded to the invitation was an elderly man. The pastor told me that four months previously this man's son had been converted. Since then he had led no fewer than eight members of his family to Christ, and this man, his father, was the ninth.

I trust that this re-issue of an old book will bring inspiration and encouragement to many personal evangelists.

J Oswald Sanders
New Zealand

1

A Heart of Compassion

He was moved with compassion (Matt. 9:36)

'Even if I were utterly selfish, and had no care for anything but my own happiness, I would choose, if I might, under God, to be a soul-winner; for never did I know perfect, overflowing, unutterable happiness of the purest and most ennobling order till I first heard of one who had sought and found the Saviour through my means. No young mother ever so rejoiced over her first-born child, no warrior was so exultant over a hard-won victory.'

These were not the extravagant words of an over-enthusiastic youth, but the measured statements of Charles Haddon Spurgeon, one of the most successful preachers of his generation in winning men and women for Christ. Only those who have never given themselves to that sacred art, would question the seeming extravagance of his statement.

Despite the fact that this 'perfect, overflowing, unutterable happiness' is within the reach of the humblest and weakest Christian, comparatively few seem sufficiently in earnest to strive after its attainment.

'A passion for souls', as a former generation termed the compassion believers should have for their fellows, is rare in our day. The great mass of Christian people appear to feel not the slightest responsibility for the eternal welfare of their fellow-men. The thought that they are their brother's keeper never seems to cross their minds. If they can ensure their own future, that is the extent of their concern.

Dr Rowland V Bingham, founder of the Sudan Interior Mission, referring to this absence of concern for the spiritual

welfare of others, had this to say: 'Today this consciousness
seems to have almost died out. The natural eye cannot see
souls. The ethical veil of society, the cloak of self-
righteousness, or the thin veneer of legal morals are
impenetrable to the natural sight, and when accompanied
with the rosy flush of youth, the glitter of prosperity and the
joys of home and social life, it is hard to realise that in the
midst of all these are lost souls. Christians, as a whole, do not
act as though they believed that anyone was lost'.

There are many reasons for this apathy, some of which
are:

Lack of conviction of man's 'lostness'

Jesus said, 'The Son of Man came to seek and to save what
was lost' (Luke 19:10), that word 'lost' being translated
'perish' in John 3:16.

Many are willing to subscribe to an orthodox creed
concerning the punishment of the wicked, but there is a
world of difference between mental assent and active
compassion. Others cannot bring themselves to believe that
our Lord's words, 'Whoever believes in the Son has eternal
life, but whoever rejects the Son will not see life, for God's
wrath remains on him' (John 3:36), are literally true.

Judge Mingins was a prominent lawyer in Philadelphia
who was well known for his rationalistic views in religion.
He was, however, won for Christ, and became equally
notable for his Christian witness.

Some time after his conversion, he was visiting one of his
former friends who said to him,

'George, I hear you are a Christian now?'

'Yes, I am', replied the judge.

'George, do you believe in God?'

'Yes.'

'And do you believe that all who do not believe in Jesus
Christ will ultimately go to hell?'

'I do, most certainly.'

'Well, George,' replied his friend, 'does Christianity dry up
all the milk of humanity in one's body as it has done in
yours?'

'What do you mean?' asked the judge.

'I mean this,' was the reply. 'You have been living under my roof for three days and three nights, knowing and believing all this, and yet you never put your hand on my shoulder, or said one word to save me.'

Against how many of us could a similar charge be laid?

The case was put even more strongly by a noted atheist of an earlier day:

'Were I a religionist, did I truly, firmly, consistently believe, as millions *say* they do, that the knowledge and the practice of religion in this life influences destiny in another, religion should be to me *everything*. I would cast aside earthly thoughts and feelings as less than vanity. Religion would be my first waking thought and my last image when sleep sunk me in unconsciousness. I would labour in her cause alone. I would not labour for the meat that perisheth, nor for treasures on earth, but only for a crown of glory in Heavenly regions where treasures and happiness are alike beyond the reach of time and chance. I would take thought for the morrow of eternity alone. I would esteem one soul gained to Heaven worth a life of suffering. There should be neither worldly prudence nor calculating circumspection in my engrossing zeal. Earthly consequences should never stay my hand nor seal my lips. I would speak to the imagination, awaken the feelings, stir up the passions, arouse the fancy. Earth, its joys and its grief, should occupy no moment of my thoughts; for these are but the affairs of a portion of eternity – so small that no language can express its comparatively infinite littleness.

'I would strive to look but on Eternity and on the immortal souls around me, soon to be everlastingly miserable or everlastingly happy. I would deem all who thought only of this world, merely seeking to increase temporal happiness and labouring to obtain temporal goods – I would deem all such pure madmen. I would go forth to the world and preach to it, in season and out of season; and my text should be, "What shall it profit a man if he gain the whole world and lose his own soul?" '

I have quoted this remarkable statement in full, because

all unwittingly, its writer has presented accurately the philosophy of life and the motivation of the Master winner of men. Read the quotation again from this perspective and see how accurately it mirrors our Lord's attitude to this world and to eternity. His life and ministry were consistent with His assertion that men who rejected salvation were eternally lost. Are ours?

In days when capital punishment was current, a chaplain escorted Charles Peace, a notorious criminal, to the scaffold. He was a forger, a burglar, a double murderer. As they walked, the chaplain endeavoured to extend to him 'the consolations of religion'. As he spoke of Christ's power to save, the condemned man turned to him saying, 'Do you believe it? Do you believe it? If I believed *that*, I would willingly crawl across England on broken glass to tell men it was true.'

Thank God it is true. But if the reality of our belief in its truth were measured by the strenuousness of our efforts to win men to Christ, then the professed belief of many could hardly be described as vital.

Lack of concern for lost men and women

The old Puritans used to speak of having 'a concern', and a meaningful expression it is. Our Lord had a concern for individuals and for the multitudes, so real and deep, that at times tears of compassion could not be restrained but ran down His cheeks.

The manly Paul besought men to be reconciled to God, 'night and day with tears.' So intense was his burden for his relatives and fellow countrymen that he wrote: 'I am not lying, my conscience confirms it in the Holy Spirit – I have great sorrow and unceasing anguish in my heart. For I could wish that I myself were cursed and cut off from Christ for the sake of my brothers, those of my own race' (Rom. 9:2,3).

William Booth-Clibborn, grandson of the founder of the Salvation Army, used to speak of 'the curse of a dry-eyed Christianity.' When a young missionary who had been invalided home was asked why he was so eager to return to his people, he replied, 'Because I cannot sleep for thinking of them.' Does sleep ever flee our eyes because of our concern for our fellows? Do tears start from our eyes as we see our cities engulfed in sin and violence and shame?

> Oh, for a passionate passion for souls,
>   Oh, for a pity that yearns.
> Oh, for a love that loves unto death,
>   Oh, for a fire that burns.
> Oh, for a pure prayer-power that prevails,
>   That pours itself out for the lost –
> Victorious prayer in the Conqueror's Name,
>   Oh, for a Pentecost.

When William C Burns, who was instrumental in revival in Murray McCheyne's Scottish parish, and later in China, was commencing his ministry, his mother met him in a sordid Glasgow street. Noticing that he was weeping, she asked him, 'Why those tears?'

'I am weeping at the sight of the multitudes in the streets, so many of whom are passing through life unsaved.'

To one of his officers who was finding his work desperately difficult and was seeing little progress, General William Booth of the Salvation Army sent the cryptic message: 'Try tears!' It worked!

Dr J H Jowett, author of the book *A Passion for Souls,* had this to say:

'The Gospel of a broken heart demands the ministry of bleeding hearts. When our sympathy loses its pang we can no longer be the servants of the passion. We can never heal the needs we do not feel. Tearless hearts can never be heralds of the passion. We must pity if we would redeem. We must bleed if we would be ministers of the saving blood.'

We are experiencing in our churches an unprecedentedly high level of scholarship in the pulpit and intelligence in the pew, but it is to be feared that culture of the heart has lagged far behind culture of the mind. Pulpit power has diminished rather than increased. If indeed one must be sacrificed on the altar of the other, less scholarship and more 'concern' would soon see a turn of the tide. But need either be sacrificed? Can they not, and should they not co-exist?

There have been many remarkable examples of very ordinary men and women entirely innocent of theology, who have demonstrated the love of the Master in such a convincing way that their appeal has been irresistible. Their obviously sincere concern for the spiritual welfare of others has produced remarkable spiritual results.

Dr·J Wilbur Chapman, the great American evangelist who initiated many simultaneous evangelistic crusades in cities around the world, tells of one such case:

'I went to hear D L Moody preach when I was a country minister, and he so fired my heart, that I went back to my country church and tried to preach as he preached, and we had really a great work of grace. It did not start immediately; and I was so discouraged, because things did not go as I thought they ought, that I called my church officers together and said: "You will have to help me." They promised to do so, and finally an old farmer rose and said: "I have not done much work in the church, but I will help you." One of the officers said to me afterwards: "Do not ask him to pray, for he cannot pray in public," and another said: "Do not ask him to speak, for he cannot speak to the edification of the people."

'Next morning we had one of those sudden snowstorms for which that part of the country is famous, and this old farmer rose and put his horse to his sleigh and started across the country, four miles to a blacksmith's shop. He hitched his horse on the outside, and went into the shop all covered with snow, and found the blacksmith alone.

'The blacksmith said: "Mr Cranmer, whatever brings you out today?" The old farmer walked to the blacksmith's bench, and putting his hand upon the man's shoulders, said: "Tom!" and the tears started to roll down his cheeks. Then with sobs choking his utterance, he said: "Tom, when your old father died, he gave you and your brother into my guardianship, and I have let you both grow to manhood and never asked you to be a Christian." That was all. He did not ask him then; he could not. He got into his sleigh and drove back home. And he did not go out again for months; he almost died from pneumonia.

'But that night in the meeting, the blacksmith stood up before my church officers and said: "Friends, I have never been moved by a sermon in my life, but when my old friend stood before me this morning, with tears and sobs, having come all through the storm, I thought it was time I considered the matter." We received him into the church, and he is a respected church officer today. *Preaching fails, singing fails, but individual concern does not fail.*'

Lack of conception of the value of a human life

Upon our conception of the value of the person to be won, will depend the strenuousness of our endeavours for his salvation. It is valid to ask the question, 'Is it really worth interfering with our enjoyment and inconveniencing ourselves to spend time seeking to lead people to Christ?' The answer will become clearer as we endeavour to arrive at a true estimate of the value and worth of a single human being.

Why will a man work much harder to recover diamonds than gravel? Because they are of so much greater value. So is it with a human life. Christ conceived the human soul to be of such transcendent value that He willingly exchanged the glories of heaven for a life of poverty, suffering, shame and death, rather than that one person should perish. In one scale He placed the world and all it could offer of fame and riches and pleasure, and in the other a human life, and He declared the scale went down on the side of the soul. This estimate of the value of a human life is implicit in His question, 'What good is it for a man to gain the whole world, yet forfeit his soul?' (Mark 8:36).

How can the value of a human life be computed?

By its nature and origin. Man was created by the will and direct act of God. 'So God created man in his own image, in the image of God he created him; male and female he created them' (Gen. 1:27). Since man is in the image of God, since life was infused into him by the very breath of God, this alone makes man a creature of eternal significance. 'The LORD

God ... breathed into his nostrils the breath of life, and man became a living being' (Gen. 2:7). No human life is insignificant.

By its powers and capacities. In the space and computer age, it seems as though the capacities and powers of man are without limit. Every year sees vast and incredible developments in technology, and mind-boggling advances in knowledge. But unfortunately so many of these remarkable discoveries and achievements have been prostituted to base uses. Almost half of the world's resources and skills are devoted to the destruction rather than to the preservation of life.

But in spite of this gloomy prognosis, man is still capable of fellowship with God, and this is the highest conceivable experience to which he can aspire.

By the duration of its existence. The Word of God teaches clearly that the human soul exists eternally. Our Lord's solemn words in Matthew 25:46 are only one affirmation of this fact: 'They will go away to eternal punishment, but the righteous to eternal life.' The human condition in the future life is determined in this life. Both the punishment of the wicked and the blessedness of the righteous are here said to be eternal.

By the cost of its redemption. When it is remembered that our salvation was procured not by the payment of shining silver or yellow gold, but by the shedding of crimson drops of the precious blood of the Son of God, this makes even the most degraded life infinitely worth saving. 'You know that it was not with perishable things such as silver and gold that you were redeemed ... but with the precious blood of Christ ... ' (1 Pet. 1:18, 19).

By the struggle required for its possession. Why is the Kingdom of Mansoul, to use Bunyan's phrase, the battleground where both God and the devil are locked in combat, one motivated by love, and the other by hatred? Because both realise and rightly appraise the potential for either good or evil of only one human life. Think of the potential of a Billy Graham and of an Adolf Hitler!

With such an experienced adversary as Satan, it is little

wonder that men are not lightly won for Christ.

If in the light of the above facts a human life is of such surpassing value, surely no trouble is too great, no labour too hard, no pain too agonising, no expense too costly to bring that person into a saving relationship with Christ.

In every age there have been those who have shown a willingness to pay a high price to bring men and women to Christ.

Impelled by a deep concern for his fellow-Muslims, Ramon Lull, the first missionary to Islam, prayed: 'To Thee O Lord, I offer myself, my wife, my children, and all I possess.' It was a costly but God-blessed act of dedication. After many years of suffering and service, he became a martyr for his Lord.

In the same class, although centuries later, was David Brainerd, the apostle to the Red Indians. 'I wanted to wear myself out in His service,' he wrote. 'I cared not how or where I lived or what hardships I went through so that I could but gain souls for Christ.'

We need a similar almost reckless dedication to Christ in the eighties if we are to make any significant spiritual impact on the contemporary world. As I write these words in Japan, I have before me a letter received from a veteran Asian missionary. He writes:

'What seems to be lacking the world over is a desire to respond to the task in places where life may possibly be thrown away in God's service. Should we not be challenging the youth of today to accept the dangers and limitations, and put their lives on the altar? Sacrifice is as much needed today as in Hudson Taylor's day.'

Such love and devotion have burned in the breasts of all who have been successful fishers of men. Their love has been reckless though calculating and prodigal, and it has borne fruit that remains.

That peerless fisher of men, D L Moody, had this to say about the value of a single human life:

'I believe that if an angel were to wing his way from earth up to Heaven, and were to say that there was one poor, ragged boy, without father or mother, with no one to care for him and teach him the way of life; and if God were to ask who among them were willing to come down to this earth and live here for fifty years and lead that one to Jesus Christ, every angel in Heaven would volunteer to go. Even Gabriel, who stands in the presence of the Almighty, would say, "Let me leave my high and lofty position, and let me have the luxury of leading one soul to Jesus Christ." There is no greater honour than to be the instrument in God's hands of leading one person out of the kingdom of Satan into the glorious light of Heaven.'

How may such a compassion be gained?

It is not the automatic or inevitable product of the human heart. It is not produced by a fresh resolution to be concerned about the spiritual welfare of others, although that is involved. It is not native to the human heart, but is an exotic plant which flourishes in close fellowship with the compassionate Christ. It will be born only in the hearts of those who use means that are adapted and calculated to stir up the mind on the subject.

It has been suggested that Paul's overwhelming concern to win men to Christ sprang from a threefold conviction. First, *a stupendous fact* that all must face – the judgment throne of God. Second, *a life-determining experience* through which all must pass – the resurrection either to life or to condemnation. Third, *a destiny* to which all things are moving – the great eternity.

If we earnestly desire to share our Master's concern, we must cherish every impression the Holy Spirit creates in our hearts. Dr J Wilbur Chapman, whom I heard preach powerfully in my youth, urged us to take the Bible and study the spiritual condition of those who are without Christ.

'Take your New Testament,' he counselled, 'and go quietly alone and read a sentence like this: "Whoever believes in Him is not condemned, but whoever does not believe stands condemned already because he has not believed in the name of God's one and only Son" (John 3:18). Then sit and think about it for ten minutes. Put your boy over against it – your girl, your wife, your husband, yourself. Then take this: "He who does not have the Son of God does not have life" (1 John 5:12). I know that a soul thus burdened generally gains its desire.'

Charles Grandison Finney, one of the greatest revivalists of all time, used to urge those who coveted this compassion and concern to 'look as it were through a telescope into hell and hear their groans; then to turn the glass upward and look into heaven, and see the saints there in their white robes, and hear them singing the song of redeeming love, and ask yourself, "Is it possible that I could prevail with God to elevate the sinner there?" Do this, and if you are not a wicked man, you will soon have as much of the spirit of prayer as your body can sustain.'

A most striking example of the urge to win men to Christ triumphing over imminent death, is that of Rev John Harper, a Scottish minister under whose ministry many were brought to Christ. He received a call to serve in the famous Moody Memorial Church in Chicago, and embarked on the supposedly unsinkable ship, the *Titanic*, to take up his appointment.

When the *Titanic* struck the fatal iceberg, Harper was one of those flung into the icy waters of the Atlantic. One sequel to that tragedy was recounted by a young Scotsman at a service in the Philpot Tabernacle in Hamilton, Canada. Here is his testimony:

'Four years ago, when I left England on board the *Titanic*, I was a careless, godless sinner. I was in this condition on the night when the terrible catastrophe took place. Very soon, with hundreds more, I found myself struggling in the cold, dark waters of the Atlantic. I caught hold of something and clung to it for dear life.

'The wail of awful distress from the perishing all around was ringing in my ears, when there floated near by me a man who, too, seemed to be clinging to something. He called to me:

"Is your soul saved?"

'I replied: "No, it is not."

"Then," said he, "Believe on the Lord Jesus Christ and you will be saved."

'We drifted apart for a few minutes, then we seemed to be driven together once more.

"Is your soul saved?" again he cried out.

"I fear it is not," I replied.

"Then if you will but believe on the Lord Jesus Christ your soul will be saved," was his further message of intense appeal to me. But again we were separated by the rolling currents. I heard him call out this message to others as they sank beneath the waters.

'There and then, with two miles of water beneath me, in my desperation I cried unto Christ to save me. I believed upon Him and I was saved. In a few minutes I heard this man of God say: "I'm going down, I'm going down,"; then: "No, no, I'm going *up*." That man was John Harper.'

When I am dying how glad I shall be
That the lamp of my life has been blazed out for Thee.
I shall be glad in whatever I gave,
Labour, or money, one sinner to save;
I shall not mind that the path has been rough,
That Thy dear feet led the way is enough.
When I am dying how glad I shall be,
That the lamp of my life has been blazed out for Thee.

2

A Prepared Instrument

'I have come to the conclusion that not everyone is called to be a soul-winner,' said a young man. That opinion would be very acceptable to those who desire to avoid witnessing for Christ, but unfortunately for them the young man's conclusion was erroneous. He would find it exceedingly difficult to substantiate his case from Scripture. So long as the Great Commission is unrevoked, so long as 'Go into all the world and preach the good news to all creation' (Mark 16:15) remains part of the divine revelation, there rests on each Christian the responsibility of obedience. Our Lord made provision for no exemptions.

Gibbon, the historian, attributes the rapid spread of Christianity, in the early stages of its inception, to the fact that 'it became the most sacred duty of a new convert to diffuse among his friends the inestimable blessing which he himself had received.'

For such a daunting and delicate task, the believer requires a special fitness if he is to be successful. What are some of the qualifications we should seek for this purpose?

An unwavering purpose

Since this ministry involves eternal issues, the wise winner of men will seek the best training and highest qualifications for the task. If a surgeon of the body requires long training, the surgeon of souls should surely endeavour to equip himself for the greatest effectiveness in his task. He will need to be convinced of the urgency of his calling.

Motivation will play an important part. If we put to ourselves the probing question, 'How will I wish I had spent my life hundreds of years from now?' what would the answer be?

Shortly after his own conversion as a result of receiving a letter of appeal from an intimate friend, Dr Henry Clay Trumbull, the first editor of the *Sunday School Times*, had faced that question, and formed a great resolve:

'The purpose I formed was, as an imperative duty, not to fail in my Christian life in confessing Christ to others. I determined that as I loved Christ, and as Christ loved souls, I would press Christ on the individual soul, so that none who were in the proper sphere of my individual responsibility or influence should lack the opportunity of meeting the question, whether or not they would individually trust and follow Christ. The resolve I made was that whenever I was in such intimacy with a soul as to be justified in choosing my theme of conversation, the theme of themes should have prominence between us, so that I might learn his need, and if possible meet it.' This life-resolve was faithfully adhered to for more than fifty years. Who can estimate its results?

If we are in earnest in our purpose to become winners of men, would not some such purpose be well-pleasing to our Master and provide the needful motivation? Shall we not place ourselves and 'all our being's ransomed powers' in the hands of our Lord, and ask Him to make us, with all our handicaps and inadequacies, fishers of men? It was to volatile Peter and his brother that Jesus said, 'Come follow Me, and I will make *you* fishers of men' (Matt. 4:19).

A confident assurance of one's own salvation

Not all Christians have a settled conviction and assurance of their salvation, and this lack of certainty gives a tentative note to their witness.

Suppose someone to whom you were presenting the claims of Christ posed the question, 'Do you really know with certainty that you yourself now have eternal life?' What would be your answer? Would you be able to ring out a resounding affirmative?

For some years, although I was a Christian, I was

tormented with doubts of my salvation. This painful problem was not resolved until I surrendered without reservation to the Lordship of Christ, and committed the control of my life to the Holy Spirit. Since then, although there have been failures, no doubt of my salvation has found even temporary hospitality in my heart.

We are surrounded by people both old and young who are longing for certainty, seeking for someone who can say, 'We speak what we know', who can speak on this subject with the conviction and authority of personal experience. 'Give us your convictions, we have enough doubts of our own' is their plea.

If we do not have this unassailable assurance, we should search the Scriptures until we are sure. It is our right to know that we are children of God if we have truly repented of our sin and have placed our full trust in the Saviour who died for our salvation. John states the case very clearly: 'I write this to you who believe in the name of the Son of God, *so that you may know that you have eternal life*' (1 John 5:13).

One of the great assurance passages is John 10:28, 29 'I have given them [my sheep] eternal life, and they shall never perish; no one can snatch them out of my hand. My Father who has given them to me is greater than all; no one can snatch them out of my Father's hand.' It would be difficult to find more reassuring words, and yet there are timid souls who say, 'I have no doubts about Christ being able to hold me, but I am afraid that I might take myself out of His hand.'

It is a striking fact that the verb in the clause 'they shall never perish' has a reflexive significance and could be translated, 'they shall not destroy themselves.' So here is further assurance for one who has truly received Christ as Saviour and Lord.

A working knowledge of the Scriptures

By this I do not mean simply a familiarity with some proof texts or with some slick formula. Those who desire to become effective fishers of men need to know what bait to use at what season. Each human being is an individual, and the passage of Scripture that brings light to one person, may be irrelevant to the needs of another. The physician does not give the same prescription to every patient. Other knowledge is valuable, this is indispensable. Nothing can take its place.

A general knowledge of the Bible, its main contents and teaching should first be gained, then how its message can best be applied in winning men to Christ must be learned. It is literally true that the Bible is the soul-winner's only kit of tools. That person will be most effective whose mind is most liberally stored with Scriptures relevant to this type of work.

When persuasion or argument fails to produce a sense of need or to bring the person to the point of decision, our recourse should be to 'the sword of the Spirit which is the Word of God.' Spirit-directed Scriptures presented in dependence on Him, will often produce the desired result. As Robert Murray McCheyne used to say, 'It is not our comment on the Word that saves, but the Word itself.' It has innate life and power.

In passing, it should be noted that the Word of God is not the sword of the believer, but of the Holy Spirit. Only when it is used in dependence on Him will it achieve redemptive results. It is the Scriptures so used that the Spirit uses to produce conviction of sin. 'When the people heard this, they were cut to the heart and said to Peter and the other apostles, Brothers, what shall we do?' (Acts 2:37). He employs the same weapon to reveal the way of salvation. 'The holy Scriptures, which are able to make you wise for salvation through faith in Christ Jesus' (2 Tim. 3:15).

A personal evangelist was speaking to a man who said he was an infidel. He quoted Luke 13:3 'No, but unless you repent you too will perish'.

'But,' protested the man, 'I do not believe the Bible'.

The evangelist repeated the same Scripture.

'It's no use quoting the Bible to me, I don't believe it,' the man replied.

'Nevertheless, this is God's Word to you, "unless you repent you will perish".'

The man went away, but in a few days he came back

asking to be shown the way of life. The Sword of the Spirit had done its work.

It is by the intelligent use of the Word of God that we can meet the excuses, overcome the objections and expose and refute the errors that abound today. We must then be men and women of *the Book* if we are to know success in this ministry.

In his monumental book *How To Work For Christ*, Dr Reuben A Torrey summarised the attitude of one who desires to be effective in the art of fishing for men. He should know how to use his Bible so as to:

1. show others their need of a Saviour;
2. show how Christ is exactly the Saviour they need;
3. show them how they can make Him their own Saviour;
4. answer difficulties and problems that hinder them from taking this step.

To these we would add that he should have a vital and active confidence in the power of the Word of God to save the most difficult individual.

One of the early students of Spurgeon's College came to the Founder one day with the lament:

'I have been preaching now for some months, and I do not think I have had a single conversion.'

'And do you expect that the Lord is going to bless you and save souls every time you open your mouth?' asked Spurgeon.

'No sir,' was the reply.

'Well then, that is why you do not get souls saved,' was the rejoinder. 'If you had believed, the Lord would have given you the blessing.'

'Without faith it is impossible to please God' is a startling assertion. This means that our faith in the Word and the power of God must be such that we will expect God to bring men to Himself through our instrumentality.

A tactful and diplomatic approach

Tact has been defined as the art of so putting ourselves in the place of others, that we can anticipate and supply their needs, and conciliate their prejudices. It is the sensitive and intuitive perception of what is proper or fitting. It includes the ability to say or do the right thing at the right time, and in such a manner that the other person is not unnecessarily angered or offended. Where this quality is lacking, it is difficult to establish rapport and an atmosphere favourable to the presentation of the gospel. Absence of tact may neutralise other splendid abilities.

Sometimes tact is exhibited in *refraining* from broaching a religious subject. On one occasion a well-known evangelist played tennis for a whole afternoon with a young man, and never mentioned religion. The young man had expected to be pressed to accept Christ, and was prepared to resent any such eventuality. In the event, the evangelist first won him to himself, and then he was able to win him to Christ. A less tactful approach would probably have alienated him.

Tact is native to some people, but is notably absent in others. 'My middle name is Frank, and I am frank by nature,' boasted a young man. What he was really confessing was his own lack of courtesy and tact.

This quality may in measure be acquired by observation, sensitivity and prayer. If we do as the old Indian chief suggested and endeavour to 'walk in other people's moccasins', we will soon establish empathy with them. We should try to imagine the tables reversed, and think how we would feel were we on the receiving end. We have gained a great deal of ground if we can make people feel at ease with us.

The story is told of a gentleman crossing the ocean who was distressed by the profanity of several men in the party. Finally, he said to them: 'Gentlemen, I believe all of you are Englishmen, and if so, you believe in fair play, do you not?'

'Certainly, that is characteristic of Britons everywhere.'

'Well, gentlemen, I notice that you have been indulging in a good deal of profanity, and I think it is my turn to swear next. Isn't that fair?'

'Of course it is,' said the others.

'Very well, remember that you are not to swear again till I have had my turn.'

'But you will not take your turn.'

'I certainly will just as soon as I see a real occasion for it.'

All this was done in a playful way, but the result of his tactful approach was that they kept their profanity bottled up for the rest of the voyage.

A habitually prayerful attitude

More will be said later about the place of prayer in winning men to Christ, but this must be listed among the elements that go to make up the fitness of the worker. In counselling young Timothy, Paul said, 'First of all [or first in order of importance] I urge that supplications, prayers, intercessions and thanksgivings be made for all men' (1 Tim. 2:1). Too often we make supplemental what God says should be fundamental. It is not enough to add a little prayer to our Christian work. Our work should grow out of our praying.

And how great our need of prayer in this delicate task! How many possibilities of error there are. What wisdom is required to discern to whom to speak, to rightly diagnose the spiritual condition of the person approached, and be able to prescribe the appropriate remedy. If the great Paul was at times compelled to cry 'Who is sufficient for these things?', we should not be surprised if we share his sense of inadequacy.

It is only as our hearts are constantly being lifted to God in prayer for guidance that the promised wisdom will be given, and we will be saved from blundering. It was because Philip was a man of faith and prayer that he was guided to an incredibly important key convert in the person of the Ethiopian eunuch (Acts 8). Only because he was sensitively in touch with God was he guided to that sincere inquirer in a most unlikely location.

When we are faced with perplexed people for whose problems we have no solution, our recourse should be to the place of prayer.

An old friend of my family, blind physically but exceptionally keen-sighted spiritually, had on many occasions unsuccessfully endeavoured to bring the light of salvation to an ignorant old woman who lived nearby. At last he came to his wits' end and left the room to pray. In his prayer he told the Lord that he had done all he could. Was there no Scripture applicable to this case? Then a verse came to his mind: 'Ye shall be my sons and daughters, saith the Lord Almighty' (2 Cor. 6:18).

'But, Lord,' he protested, 'that has nothing to do with salvation.' Try as he would, he could get no other message, so he quoted this verse to his friend.

'Does it say that?' she eagerly asked. 'I thought it was all for men – "If any *man* thirst" – but this verse says: "Ye shall be my sons and *daughters*."' Merely human wisdom would never have suggested this verse as the solution of the old woman's difficulties, but through prayer her friend was given the unerring counsel of the Spirit of God. He often used this incident as an illustration of the absolute necessity of depending on the Spirit of God for the appropriate message.

The five previous qualifications for the winner of men are all desirable and valuable, but there is one that is indispensable if we are to become really effective in this field of endeavour.

The enduement of power

Among the last recorded words of our Lord to His disciples was His charge, 'I am going to send you what my Father has promised; but stay in the city until you have been clothed with power from on high' (Luke 24:49). Just before His ascension He assured His disciples, 'You will receive power when the Holy Spirit comes on you; and you will be my witnesses' (Acts 1:8).

Without this divine empowering, one may have formed an unwavering purpose, enjoy a satisfying assurance of salvation, possess a knowledge of Scripture, be very tactful and prayerful, and yet not be successful in the divine art of winning men and women to Christ. With it, the value of all this equipment and training is immeasurably enhanced.

From a study of the biographies of great men and women who have been singularly successful in this ministry, there emerges the fact that in almost every case there came a crisis, a new and more complete surrender to the Lordship of Christ, and a new enduement of the Holy Spirit that equipped them for the task entrusted to them. They discovered that it was the Holy Spirit Himself who was their power for service.

If the reader knows little of His empowering in personal experience, a careful study of the teaching of Scripture on this subject would pay valuable dividends.

Observe the tremendous transformation evident in Peter's life after he had been so endued. He preached with a passion, a logic, a fearlessness, a convicting power to which he was previously a stranger. His words from then on left saving impressions on the minds of his hearers. We should seek and appropriate this promised enduement, without which our most earnest endeavours will prove abortive.

> I am trusting Thee for power,
> Thine can never fail,
> Words which Thou Thyself wilt give me,
> Must prevail.

F R Havergal

3

The Power of Prayer

If it is our genuine desire to be used in cooperation with the Holy Spirit in leading men and women to faith in Christ, we must in some degree master the holy art of intercession. If the Master wept and prayed over the lost, then His servant should partake of His spirit. Prayer should always have an important place in our programme, since the salvation of a soul is not a human, but a divine work, and it is prayer that releases the power of God.

Since prayer fills so important a role, it follows that whatever hinders us in its exercise must go. The issues involved are so great that it is worth paying any price to render our prayers more effective.

If we expect God to answer our prayers, *we must be sure we are standing on praying ground.* The psalmist declared categorically: 'If I had cherished sin in my heart, the Lord would not have listened' (Ps. 66:18) – let alone answered my prayer. That clearly means that we are on praying ground only when we have sincerely renounced all sins of which the Holy Spirit has convicted us, and resolved every controversy between ourselves and God. Have you done this? The Holy Spirit will give the assurance when the last thing has been dealt with.

It is when we have a heart that has been cleansed, *a heart that is at leisure from itself* and its own concerns, that God will be able to entrust us with a deep burden for the salvation of others. Paul likened this to a woman travailing in birth, a figure that illustrates the intensity and costliness of prevailing prayer. He was a shining example of what he taught: 'I speak the truth in Christ, I am not lying, my conscience confirms it in the Holy Spirit – I have great sorrow and unceasing anguish in my heart. For I could wish that I myself were cursed and cut off from Christ for the sake of my brothers, those of my own race' (Rom. 9:1-3).

Count Zinzendorf, the German nobleman who founded the Moravian community that conducted one of the greatest missionary enterprises of all time, was deeply concerned, as a young man, for the spiritual welfare of a few girls ranging in age from ten to thirteen, whose spiritual education had become his responsibility.

'He observed that though their demeanour was blameless,' the record runs, 'and their intellectual grasp of truth satisfactory, yet no evidence of a heart knowledge of God appeared among them. This weighed on him and led him to earnestly intercede for them. Cultured, wealthy young nobleman that he was, he was not above taking thought for the spiritual welfare of a few girls. More intense grew his concern, culminating at last in such a season of truly energised prayer as produced a most extraordinary effect.'

The blessing he desired for his class came, and much more too, for this was the beginning of the remarkable work among the Moravians which bore fruit in their widespread missionary work in a day when missionaries were few.

The prayer of the fisher of men for himself will be threefold. First, he should pray *for moral courage to speak for Christ* when suitable opportunity offers. Our Lord knows that in the world which rejected and crucified Him, it will never be easy to speak for Him. For some temperaments the fear of man is an almost insuperable barrier, and the apostles were not exempt from this inhibiting fear. How did they overcome it? They prayed! 'Now Lord, consider their threats and enable your servants to speak your word with great boldness ... and they were all filled with the Holy Spirit and spoke the word of God boldly' (Acts 4:29-31). We will be able, after prayer, to do what we never could have done without it.

It may encourage fearful hearts to know that one of the most successful personal evangelists gave this testimony:

'People often say to me, "It is easy for you to do it." I want to say that I never find it easy, especially to start with. From nearly half a century of practice, I find it as difficult to speak

about it at the end as at the beginning. I never speak to a
person about Christ without being reminded by Satan that I
am in danger of doing harm by introducing the subject just
now.

'We may make mistakes, but no mistake is so bad as the
fatal mistake of not making an honest endeavour.'

The next prayer would be *for guidance as to whom to
approach and when.* To speak to people indiscriminately
and without inner conviction and guidance can be hurtful
both to the worker and to those whom he addresses.
Obviously it is not God's intention that we speak to everyone
we meet, although He does expect us to be willing to do so.

One noted preacher and soul-winner said that he used to
feel condemned unless he spoke to everyone he met. He
obtained release from this bondage when he made it a matter
of prayer that God would show him the ones to whom to
witness. There are many with whom we come in contact, for
whom God has no message at the moment. If we cultivate the
habit of constantly looking to the Lord for an indication of
His will, He will guide us when to speak and when to be
silent.

A student of mine when in Bible College made it a practice
to sit on a seat in the park and prayerfully wait until another
man came along. He would then engage him in conversation
about Christ. He told me that he spoke with eighty men in
this way, and he became a skilful winner of men.

Finally, having established contact, we will need *guidance
as to what to say.* The inexperienced fisher of men should
bear in mind that every soul-winner was once as inexperienced as he is, and had to learn through experience.
Isaiah testified that he learned the art through prayer and
communion with God. 'The Sovereign LORD has given me
an instructed tongue, to know the word that sustains the
weary. He wakens me morning by morning, wakens my ear
to listen like one being taught' (50:4). God knows whether
the message should be one of love or repentance or warning.

If God is calling us to speak to someone, then we can safely
trust him for the message. He knows every need of the
human heart, and has given the Holy Spirit to bring the

appropriate Scriptures to remembrance, as He did with Peter on the Day of Pentecost. 'He will remind you of everything I have said to you,' was His promise to Peter (John 14:26).

The worker's prayer for those to be won will also be threefold. First, *that rapport may speedily be established, and hostility or indifference be broken down*. Unless the ministry of the Holy Spirit precedes that of the worker, he will try in vain to storm the citadel of the human heart. It is persistent, believing prayer that will break down the most determined opposition.

Next, *that the soil of the heart may be prepared for the sowing of the seed*. The parable of the sower makes it clear that it is only when the seed is sown in good soil that there will be a harvest. This is the work of the Holy Spirit. 'When he comes, he will convict the world of guilt in regard to sin and of righteousness and judgment' (John 16:8). He does this important work of conviction – ploughing up the soil of the human heart – in answer to prayer.

Lastly, *that the soul may be liberated from the power of Satan*. It is just here that the battle for Mansoul is joined. Prayer of this kind is a spiritual warfare. Satan, who is 'the strong man' of Matthew 12:29, has bound every son of Adam, and contests their deliverance from his clutches every inch of the way. It is by the prayer of faith alone that the strong man can be bound by the stronger than he, and his captives set free.

'Real prayer is opposing a great spiritual force to the onslaught of evil, and asking God to put into operation the work done by His Son on the cross, which was not only the redemption of man, but the defeat of the prince of this world.' It is for us to learn under the Spirit's guidance how to bring our conquering Lord's victory on Calvary into play in our own fields of battle. Revelation 12:11 gives us the secret of victory over Satan – 'They overcame him by the blood of the Lamb and by the word of their testimony; they did not love their lives so much as to shrink from death.' Let us follow in their train.

Our praying is likely to be futile unless it is *definite in its aim*. The marksman aims at only one spot. After he has fired his rifle, he knows whether or not he has hit his target. Our prayers should be no less definite and specific, and we will know whether or not they have been answered. We should not sweep our unanswered prayers under the carpet, but search out the reasons for non-answer.

We should *pray for specific people*. But for whom? Here again the Holy Spirit comes to our aid. As we pray, He will lay a burden on our hearts for certain people who are or will be within our sphere of influence.

God laid such a burden for two persons on the heart of a pastor in his first pastorate. He prayed for them faithfully throughout that pastorate, but neither was converted. For some years he continued to pray for them daily, and when later conducting an evangelistic campaign in that city, both accepted Christ the same night. His was a Spirit-inspired prayer that proved the validity of Paul's words: 'The Spirit helps us in our weakness. We do not know what we ought to pray, but the Spirit himself intercedes ... for the saints in accordance with God's will' (Rom. 8:26, 27).

Then, too, *our praying should be systematic*. 'The Lord is a God of system' (Isa. 30:18 margin), and His children should be like Him. Method in prayer will help to create that perseverance which is so often absent from our prayers. We pray, and run away. 'Foolish boys that knock at the door in wantonness, will not stay until some one cometh to open them,' said an old Puritan, 'but a man that hath business will knock and knock again until his call is answered.' Read Luke 11:9, 10. Let us not hang up the telephone receiver before the answer comes over the heavenly wires. 'Jesus told his disciples a parable to show them that they should always pray and not give up' (Luke 18:1).

We may comply with all the foregoing conditions, but unless we have a *believing heart* our prayers will be in vain. 'Without faith it is impossible to please God, because anyone who comes to him *must believe* that he exists and that he rewards those who earnestly seek him' (Heb. 11:6). 'But when he asks he must believe and not doubt ... That man should not think that he will receive anything from the Lord' (James 1:6, 7). Let us not dishonour God through disbelieving Him. Expect Him to do the unexpected.

Many have proved the value of using a notebook in which are entered the names of people for whom the Holy Spirit has impressed them to pray, space being left for the insertion of the date, and the date of the answer. This will help in securing definiteness of aim and perseverance in prayer. If the reader does not have such a prayer remembrance, begin one now, and keep these people constantly before the Lord in prayer. Praying prepares the way for witnessing, and soon you will have the surpassing joy of entering the date of answer opposite some of the names.

It is doubtful if anyone is saved apart from the prevailing prayer of some concerned believer. Writing of his own conversion, J Hudson Taylor, founder of the China Inland Mission, said:

'Little did I know at that time what was going on in the heart of my dear mother, 70 or 80 miles away. She rose from the dinner-table that afternoon with an intense yearning for her boy's conversion, and feeling that a special opportunity was afforded her of pleading with God on my behalf, she went to her room and turned the key in the door, resolved not to leave that spot until her prayers were answered. Hour after hour that dear mother pled for me, until at length she could pray no longer, but was constrained to praise God for that which His Spirit had taught her was already accomplished – the conversion of her only son.

'When our mother came home a fortnight later, I was the first to meet her at the door, and to tell her I had such glad news to give. I can almost feel that dear mother's arms around my neck as she pressed me to her bosom and said, "I know, my boy; I have been rejoicing for a fortnight in the glad tidings you have to tell me."

"Why," I asked in surprise, "has Amelia broken her promise? She said she would tell no one."

'My dear mother assured me that it was not from any human source that she had learned the tidings, and went on to tell the little incident above. You will agree with me that it would be strange indeed if I were not a believer in the power of prayer.'

Lord, teach us so to pray!

4

Aids in Counselling

We have reviewed the need of a genuine compassion and concern for our fellows, and some of the necessary qualifications, but the art of winning men to Christ can be learned only by doing it.

In writing a textbook for students in the Bible Institute of Los Angeles, Dr T C Horton said: 'Men are not born soul-savers, but are made. There is a widespread mis-apprehension in the minds of most Christians concerning responsibility for this work. They seem to think that *some* people are so called, but that the obligation is not universal; that it is work which one *may do* or not do as they choose. This is false, unscriptural and illogical. Soul-saving is the greatest work in the world, and is committed to every believer. All may have the joy of doing it who *give themselves* to it, and all who fail to do so are recreant to a holy trust, and will soon be the poorer throughout eternity.' If this is true, then let us give ourselves to this privileged ministry with abandon.

Here is some advice, both positive and negative, which will guide us in our endeavours:

Do believe God's promise of wisdom. 'If any of you lacks wisdom, he should ask God who gives generously to all, and it will be given him' (James 1:5). Some hold back from this work because they feel ill-equipped, and are sure they could never succeed. This promise is for such people. Often stammering words uttered in genuine concern have achieved more than flowery language. Even if we seem to have failed or have made mistakes, where there is genuine and prayerful concern, God can bless even our blunders.

Do claim from God deliverance from the fear of man. It is incontrovertible that 'the fear of man brings a snare'. This is perhaps one of the main reasons why many, especially those who are of a timid or retiring nature, do not embark on this ministry. But there is deliverance from this bondage.

A Christian lawyer with whom I used to work as a young man was a fearless witness for Christ. One day, groaning under the bondage of fear of what others would think or say, I ventured to ask him if he had always been bold in his witness.

He replied that he had been as timid as anyone, until one day he could stand it no longer. He fell on his knees with his Bible open at Psalm 34:4: 'I sought the Lord, and He answered me and *delivered me from all my fears.*' 'Lord, you did this for David,' he prayed, 'do it for me now.' From that moment his timidity was replaced by a holy boldness.

So long as we are in bondage to the opinions of others, our work will be circumscribed and hampered. There are many who fail to engage in aggressive soul-winning, through fear of being thought peculiar. Do claim deliverance from this satanic fear. God will give a full deliverance to the most timid and fearful soul who dares to claim it.

Do keep your eyes open for opportunities. I have found myself surrounded with opportunities *when willing to seize them*; but when I was unwilling, no opportunities seemed to present themselves. Doubtless, there were just as many, but I was blind to them. We can be so occupied with what we consider 'bigger things' that we neglect to speak to our milkman, baker, butcher or postman.

The following confession by a missionary secretary appeared some years ago in the *Missionary Review of the World*: 'I was helping to get up a big convention, and was full of enthusiasm over making the session a success. On the opening day, my aged father, who came as a delegate to the convention, sat with me at luncheon at the hotel. He listened sympathetically to my glowing accounts of the great features that were to be. When I paused for breath, he leaned towards me and said, whilst his eye followed the stately movements of the head waiter: "Daughter, I think that big head waiter over there is going to accept Jesus Christ. I've been talking to him about his soul." I almost gasped. I had been too busy planning for a great missionary convention. I had no time to think of the soul of the head waiter.

'When we went out to my apartment, a Negro man was washing the apartment windows. Jim was honest and trustworthy, and had been a most satisfactory helper in my home. Only a few moments passed before I heard my father talking earnestly with Jim about his personal salvation, and a swift accusation went to my heart as I realised that I had known Jim for years, and had never said a word to him of salvation.

'A carpenter came in to repair a door. I awaited his going with impatience to sign his work ticket, for my ardent soul longed to be back at my missionary task. Even as I waited I heard my father talking with the man about the door he had just fixed, and then simply and naturally leading the conversation to the only door into the Kingdom of God.

'A Jew lives across the street. I had thought that possibly I would call on the folks who lived in the neighbourhood – some time – but I had my hands so full of missionary work the calls had never been made; but, as they met on the street, my father talked with my neighbour of the only Saviour of the world.

'A friend took us out to ride. I waited for my father to get into the car, but in a moment he was up beside the chauffeur, and in a few minutes I heard him talking earnestly with the man about the way of salvation. When we reached home he said: "You know, I was afraid I might never have another chance to speak to the man."

'The wife of a prominent railway man took him out to ride in her elegant limousine. "I am glad she asked me to go," he said, "for it gave me an opportunity of talking with her about her salvation. I think no one had ever talked with her before."

'Yet these opportunities had come to me also, and had passed by as ships in the night, while I strained my eyes to catch sight of a larger sail on a more distant horizon. I could but question my own heart whether my passion was for souls, or for success in getting up conventions.'

Comment is needless. We are surrounded by opportunities – in our homes, in the church, in the Sunday School, among our friends, relatives, neighbours, employees, fellow-workmen, on trains or cars, in parks or on the streets, if only we are willing to avail ourselves of them. *Do* take advantage of your opportunities.

Do endeavour to bring the person to a point of decision. It is not sufficient to state the way of salvation clearly. We are working towards a verdict for our Master.

After hearing a convincing sermon on 'The Power of the Cross', a layman said to the preacher: 'I heard you preach last Sunday; I was greatly moved. But if you will permit me, I should like to offer this criticism. I am a business man at the head of a large concern; we send out many salesmen. If one of my salesmen went into a prospective customer's place of business, talked as convincingly as you did last Sunday about the fine quality of our goods, and then walked away without trying to get an order, we would discharge him.' The minister felt that he was rebuked; that the layman was right; that although he was pleading for a verdict, he sought no announcement of it; and although he was 'selling goods' he did not try to get an order.

Do learn to speak the language of the ordinary man and avoid religious jargon and clichés. People today are not reading the Bible or listening to sermons. Their ideas are largely being shaped by radio and TV, and the writings of humanistic philosophers. Words expressing the great doctrines of our faith are simply not understood today as our fathers knew them.

Do purpose to win at least one person to Christ. You might well shrink from the task if you were asked to win twenty, but could you not win one? Have you ever honestly tried this? Don't say, 'I can't!' for God never requires us to do something we can't do. Ask the Lord to lay one soul upon your heart, and then lay yourself out to win that one. Incalculable possibilities lie in this purpose.

Dwight L Moody, who later became a great world evangelist, the Billy Graham of his day, was reared in a Unitarian environment, went to Boston at an early age, was induced to join a Sunday School class, and was led to a definite acceptance of Christ through the faithful personal persuasion of the teacher of that class, Edward Kimball. When Andrew brought Peter to Jesus, he brought through Peter 3,000 souls on the day of Pentecost; and when Edward Kimball brought Moody to Jesus, he brought, through Moody, a million people to the Saviour. One single person is worth it all, but infinite possibilities are wrapped up in *every* human life.

But the converse, alas, is equally true. Consider the negative side. Joseph Smith, who later became the leader of the Mormon Church, lived in a neglected home in a certain country community. A farmer on his way to church passed that home every Sunday, but he never asked the poor lad to accompany him, or even to attend Sunday School. The sad consequences of that failure will never be blotted out. Unnumbered lives have been blighted and homes ruined.

In *every* community there are potential Moodys, potential Billy Grahams, and also, alas! *potential Joseph Smiths!* There may be one or the other *in your own home*, or in your neighbour's home. Do seek to win at least one soul for your Lord.

In order to crystallise this purpose for you, will you here and now add your name to the following suggested pledge?

Win One Soul

I will seek, with God's help, to win one soul each year, and endeavour to get them to do the same.

Name ....
Date ....

On the negative side, *don't let your ultimate objective be too apparent*. The skilful fisherman conceals his hook and chooses his bait carefully. It could be counterproductive to approach someone with a bundle of tracts in one's hand, or with a big Bible under one's arm.

Don't attempt, as a rule, to aproach more than one person at a time. Your 'prospect' will be unlikely to open his heart and disclose his real difficulty in the presence of others.

Don't be drawn into argument, or you are liable to be side-tracked from your main objective. Keep to the point. Few have been argued into salvation. There are of course times when it is necessary to defend one's position, but care must be taken lest in winning the argument we lose the one we are seeking to win. Usually what keeps people from accepting Christ as Saviour is not the logical or intellectual difficulties, but unwillingness to surrender heart and will to Him.

Don't attract undue attention to yourself or your experience. A testimony can at times prove very effective but it should be Christ-centred, not self-centred. The Holy Spirit will cooperate when we endeavour to attract people to our Lord.

Don't monopolise the conversation. A compulsive talker will often defeat his own ends by preventing the one to whom he is talking from sharing his problems and views. If your friend has a lot to say, be a good listener. He will stop talking sooner or later, and then the worker's chance will come to present Christ. This can be done more effectively if the person's viewpoint or problems have first been discovered.

Don't, as a general rule, deal with people of the opposite sex. This area is so delicate that motivation can become mixed. There will undoubtedly be times when it will be right and proper to speak with those of the opposite sex about Christ, but it is not desirable for a young man or a young woman to make a habit of this. Wherever possible, pass them on to someone of their own sex for counsel.

Don't, as a rule, choose a person much older than you to counsel. An experienced Christian more nearly in their age bracket will be more likely to meet and answer their questions and problems.

Don't rely only on your own ability, powers of persuasion or Bible knowledge. Paul indicated his reliance on His Lord when he said, 'I can do everything through him who gives me strength' (Phil. 4:13). Maintain an attitude of constant dependence on the Holy Spirit and expect Him to wield His sword.

Don't unduly multiply texts and illustrations. Some well-meaning workers bombard their hearer with a multiplicity of texts that only serve to confuse them. Have three or four verses in mind that clearly reveal the need and prescribe the remedy. One or two pertinent illustrations may shed light on the path. It is often advisable to answer questions and difficulties from the Scriptures rather than from one's own experience.

Don't disagree violently with any views expressed. Find some alternative to blunt disagreement. Say, for example, 'Well now, look at the matter like this', or 'There is something in what you say, but . . .', or 'I quite see your point of view'. This keeps the channel of communication open.

Don't be unduly familiar with the inquirer. Putting a hand on the arm or shoulder or putting one's arm around them sometimes arouses resentment.

Don't break in when someone else is counselling an inquirer. Never interrupt at a point of crisis. You may feel you could do better, and that may be so, but this would not be the time to do it. Similarly, do not allow others to interrupt you at such a time.

Don't hurry or do shoddy work. Since eternal issues are at stake, we must not be careless or negligent in our approach.

Don't be discouraged by apparent failure. Remember that it is only the tip of the iceberg that is visible above the ocean surface. When failure is experienced, conduct a post-mortem and ask the Lord to reveal the cause of failure, and show you how the mistake can be avoided in the future. Failures can thus become stepping-stones to future success. In any case, we can be confident that the Word of God does not fail.

Keep out of sight. An experienced angler gave this instruction as a golden maxim: 'Let the trout see the angler, and the angler will see no trout.' How prone we are to make ourselves too prominent.

Don't forget that your only weapons are 'the sword of the Spirit which is the word of God' and 'praying in the Spirit on all occasions' (Eph. 6:17, 18). Make full use of both.

5

Making the Diagnosis

Reference was made in a previous chapter to the fact that we are surrounded by opportunities for witness that we too often fail to seize. This theme deserves further development. Bishop Westcott maintained that 'all our natural endowments, all our personal histories, all our contrasted circumstances, are so many opportunities for peculiar work.' But these opportunities must be embraced.

In the studio of an ancient Greek sculptor stood a rather peculiar piece of work. In was a statue, the hair of whose head was thrown around to cover the face; on each foot there was a wing, and the statue was standing on its toes. The visitor asked for its name, and the sculptor said it was 'Opportunity'.

'Why is its face veiled?' he asked.

'Because men seldom know her when she comes to them,' was the reply.

'And why does she stand upon her toes, and why the wings?'

'Because,' said the sculptor, 'when once she is gone, she can never be overtaken.'

A prominent Christian worker entered a store and something said, 'Speak to the clerk; speak to the clerk!' Instead of doing it he went out. But the voice kept speaking for an hour, and at last he went back and asked for the clerk. The proprietor said, 'We had an awful tragedy here a few moments ago. Immediately after you went out the clerk that waited on you went into the back room and shot a bullet through his brain. He is back there now if you wish to see him.'

So through failure to respond to the insistent promptings of the Holy Spirit, opportunity was irretrievably lost. Each day there are people around us who might be led to Christ if we were spiritually sensitive and obedient.

Where may we find such opportunities for witness?

In the home

A friend of the author, who was anxious to serve her Lord, saw in the man who came to attend to her gas supply a candidate for eternity. She faced him with the claims of Christ and had the joy of leading him into salvation. Another friend saw and seized a similar opportunity with the milkman who came weekly to collect his account, with a similar happy result.

Are not we all faced with similar opportunities? Parents have innumerable opportunities of bringing their children to the feet of the Saviour. A housemaid in the home of a Syrian general brought salvation to her master (2 Kings 5:1-5). Lord Shaftesbury, the great philanthropist, was brought to Christ through one of his housemaids. Andrew brought his brother Peter to Christ. Let us never neglect the opportunities for witness that present themselves to us right in our own homes.

In Sunday School, Bible Class, Youth Group

It is not sufficient for the teacher or leader to present the way of salvation to the class *en masse*. It is his privilege and duty to lovingly press the claims of Christ on the individual member, preferably not in the presence of others. The leader's own home would be a suitable venue. One leader known to me began a Bible Class for his schoolboys. Today thirty of them are Christians. Another friend with large business interests has seen twelve members of his Bible Class become missionaries.

At social gatherings

I recently attended a novel social gathering. Several Christian couples were asked to invite non-Christian couples in whom they were interested to a very beautiful house for the evening. Most of those who came were strangers to each other.

The host and hostess were proprietors of a fashionable restaurant, and employed Chinese staff. After the guests arrived, we were each presented with a Chinese 'fortune cookie'. Inside was a slip of paper with a clue, and we had to discover our partner. When that was done, we were divided into small teams and told we were to make and cook our own hors d'oeuvres – a Chinese egg roll and a wonton. The materials were all ready, and there was great hilarity as we tried our skill at the unaccustomed task. Needless to say by the time the meal was over the guests were no longer strangers and we moved naturally into an informal gathering when it was my privilege to open the Scriptures to them. Some of those non-Christian couples are now attending regular Bible studies.

There are many imaginative ways in which a social gathering can be turned into an effective sphere of witness.

In the church

The church should provide the most fruitful opportunities for winning people to Christ, although this is not always the case. Trained counsellors, seated in reserved places in the sanctuary, can be alert to discern evidences of interest in those present. A friendly inquiry as to how they have enjoyed the service can open the way for a conversation on spiritual topics. An invitation to a visitor to come to one's home is a natural way to establish spiritual contact.

In travel

Journeys on buses, trains, ships and planes will afford the alert Christian with opportunities of making the Saviour known. The writer has had remarkable instances of the Lord's leading in conversation with fellow-travellers.

When crossing the Atlantic, Sir George Williams, founder of the YMCA, made a point of speaking to every person on board the liner from captain to engineer, from gambler in the lounge to emigrant in the steerage. The remarkable fact is that he said he could not recollect a single instance when he received a rude or mocking retort.

Among people of one's own class

A nurse will be able most readily to reach another nurse, a soldier another soldier. An invalid would have an excellent point of contact with a shut-in. Christian athletes have formed their own association with a view to witnessing to fellow athletes, and with much success.

The personal evangelist should covet and cultivate an easy manner of approach to spiritual subjects, for it requires tact and skill to turn the conversation from secular to sacred subjects. He must be always ready to converse about Christ, and a few suggestions as to how best to do this follow.

Be natural in manner and in tone of voice. Let it be seen that your religion forms a joyous and natural part of your everyday life. Some onlookers at an open-air service remarked: 'They don't seem to get very much kick out of it.' Let us show by our manner that we really enjoy Christ.

Study the art of diverting conversation to spiritual topics as did Jesus with the woman of Samaria. A student was taking a photograph of a tourist ship as she lay alongside the wharf. A youth standing nearby volunteered the statement, 'I suppose she's as safe as hell.' The student immediately asked him if he considered hell safe, diverted the conversation into spiritual channels, and led him to Christ.

A man was endeavouring to sell a stain-remover to a Christian housewife. After buying it (an important element in the approach), she said: 'I know something which will remove stains too.' 'What is that?' he enquired. The door was now open and she replied, 'The blood of Jesus Christ', and proceeded to introduce him to her Saviour.

Have something to offer, whether it be a tract, an invitation to a service, or a Gospel. Supposing the tract was *God's Way of Salvation*, the person could be approached thus: 'Would you mind accepting a little booklet to read?' spoken with a cheery smile. 'It tells God's way of salvation.

Do you know God's way of salvation?' 'I'm not sure if I do.' 'Would you mind if I told you?' If the tract was *The Reason Why*, the worker could say: 'This little booklet tells the reason why no one can afford to be without Christ. I wonder if you know Christ as your Saviour. Do you?' In some such way as this it is easy to enter on a conversation which may lead to the salvation of a soul.

It is often helpful to *put the person under some obligation to you*, as by lending your newspaper on the train or bus, or doing some other little service which will create a spirit of comradeship.

Sometimes a direct question can be introduced into a conversation. 'Are you a Christian?' could lead to a successful conversation.

On one occasion a zealous soul-winner addressed this question to two ladies. 'Certainly,' they replied.

'Have you been born again?' he asked.

'This is Boston,' said the ladies, 'and you know we don't believe in that doctrine here.'

He immediately produced his Bible and showed what God has to say on the subject. In a short time they were on their knees. That evening one of the ladies told her husband of her encounter with the evangelist.

'I wish I had been there,' said the man.

'What would you have done?' asked his wife.

'I would have told him to go about his business.'

'But if you had been there, you would have said he *was* about his business.'

An accurate diagnosis

The first task of the physician is to correctly diagnose the case, or his prescription will be at random. So with the soul-physician. The doctor asks questions so couched as to reveal the inward condition, and the physician of souls must do the same. The questions at first may be general, but must proceed to the particular. Is he a spiritual drop-out, a non-witnessing Christian, ignorant of the simple plan of salvation, ensnared by some cult, clinging to some sin, sceptical, or hindered by some honest difficulties? This can be discovered only by careful and tactful questioning.

Commence by saying: 'Have you ever made a decision for Christ?' If the answer is in the affirmative, next ascertain whether he had really experienced the new birth. If the answer is again in the affirmative, enquire what has led to his present unsatisfactory condition. But if, on the other hand, it has been merely a 'decision', without any real change in life-style, speak as though the person was unconverted, and point him to Christ. In subsequent chapters, instruction will be given as to how to treat those who have honest difficulties, or make dishonest excuses.

The following story shows the importance of correct diagnosis. Let me give it in the counsellor's own words. 'I was asked to counsel a certain man after a service. Before I reached him, however, someone else began to talk to him and I turned to others. Later I saw the other counsellor leaving him. Approaching him I said: "Have you settled the great question?" "No," interjected the counsellor, "he is going away unsaved because he will not give his heart to God."

"What is the trouble?" I enquired. I soon surmised that it was not a case of stubborn unwillingness to yield to Christ, but rather a lack of confidence in his ability to make the surrender real. I told him that if he would surrender, Christ would enable him to make the surrender good. I then suggested that we kneel, and that he follow me sentence by sentence while I led in prayer. He said he did not know whether he could honestly do it.

"Follow me as far as you can and then stop," I replied. He consented, and we knelt down together and I led him in a committal to Christ as strong and complete as I knew how to make it, going cautiously, of course, at first, but making it stronger as I saw his willingness to follow. When we arose, he told the first person he met that he had accepted Christ as his Saviour.' The first counsellor failed because he had made a false diagnosis, mistaking the man's lack of confidence for stubborn wilfulness.

It should be stressed that we must sincerely seek the

wisdom of the Holy Spirit to pierce any mask or veneer, and get right to the heart of the problem. The intricacy of the human heart is such that we need insight from above to make an accurate diagnosis.

The diagnosis, of course, must be followed by the prescribing of the appropriate remedy, a subject we will cover in the next chapter.

6

Writing the Prescription

Correct diagnosis must be followed by accurate prescription. There is an appropriate remedy for every ill of the human heart. The same medicine will not cure every ailment, and we must be in sensitive touch with the Great Physician if we are to learn to prescribe aright. Once again we will need to ask wisdom from above (James 1:7).

In the course of our counselling we will meet various classes of people whose needs are widely divergent. We will first consider the needs of

Professing Christians

Among these are *people whose Christian experience has been unsatisfactory*. First try to find out the reasons for such a condition. The causes of spiritual decline are very much the same in most cases – neglect of prayer, Bible study and witnessing; flirting with the world; toleration of certain sins; entertaining doubt; lack of assurance of salvation. Let us consider how we can prescribe for some of these conditions.

Neglect of prayer

This is a regrettably common neglect among Christians, even with those who would readily concede its importance. Along with neglect of the Bible, this is one of the most fruitful causes of decline. But prayer is the Christian's vital breath.

Some time ago the writer met a fine young man, truly converted and anxious to walk with God, and yet who was making no progress. In response to a question he admitted that he did not regularly read and pray. On having the part which prayer and Bible-reading play in the Christian life explained to him, he said: 'I did not know, and no one ever told me, that this was necessary to growth in the Christian life.' It was touching to hear him pray as though God had given him a great revelation. Never take it for granted that the young convert will automatically read and pray. Instruct him on this point.

Endeavour to find the reason for the lack of prayer and suggest possible causes and cure (James 4:2). Show the value of a Quiet Time (Matt. 6:6). Quote Christ's example (Matt. 14:13,23; Mark 1:35), as well as that of other saints (Ps. 55:17; Dan. 6:10; Matt. 26:41; Eph. 6:18).

Neglect of the Bible
Show the place the Bible must hold in the life of the happy Christian. Ask why it is that it seems so difficult to find time for Bible reading and prayer, and yet time is found for everything else we really want to do. Suggest that one reason is that the devil knows if he can prevent this he will paralyse the whole of the believer's life of service. Use 1 Peter 2:2; James 1:21, 22; 2 Timothy 3:15-17 – a passage which shows the part the Bible plays in saving from error and equipping for service; Ps. 119:9, 130 – one of the secrets of victory; Ps. 1:1, 2; John 5:38, 39; Acts 17:11; John 8:31.

Neglect of witnessing
Many Christians never experience the full joy of salvation because open confession of Christ has never been made (Rom. 10:9, 10). Ascertain if the inquirer has ever done this, and if he is still witnessing. If not, point out that this could be at the root of his unsatisfactory experience. One who is ashamed of Jesus cannot be His really happy disciple.

At an evangelistic meeting a young woman responded to the invitation. She was counselled but went away uncertain as to whether anything had happened. On reaching her lodging, she thought that she would write to her mother and tell her what had transpired. She said that as soon as she put pen to paper, the joy of assurance of salvation flooded her heart (Matt. 10:32, 33). If the reason for non-witness is fear of ridicule or persecution, use John 12:42, 43. Encourage the inquirer to launch out into witnessing, using Daniel 12:3; Proverbs 11:30; Philippians 4:13.

Compromise with the world
Since James 4:4 is true, and 'friendship with the world is enmity with God', it naturally follows that the Christian who is on good terms with the world is not on good terms with God, and *vice versa*. God has commanded us to be separate from the world and not to love it (1 John 2:15-17; 2 Cor. 6:14-7:1; Matt. 6:24; Luke 8:14). Bring the inquirer to the point where he will make a definite and final break with the world (1 Cor. 6:19, 20; 8:13; Col. 3:17; 1 Tim. 4:6; 1 Cor. 6:12).

It would be wise to point out the distinction between *isolation* from the world, and *insulation* from the world. We cannot win people to Christ if we isolate ourselves from them, but if we are walking in the Spirit we will be insulated from wordly influences. Believers are the salt of the earth, but salt cannot fulfil its function if there is no contact.

Lack of assurance of salvation
This may arise from simple ignorance – no one has shown them from Scripture that they can know with certainty before death that they possess eternal life. In such a case use 1 John 5:10-13, stressing the last verse. Other relevant passages are John 1:12; 3:36; 5:24; Acts 13:39. Clarify what believing in Christ really means, and satisfy yourself that this saving belief is present.

Sometimes, however, the lack of assurance stems from toleration of sin. Find out what is hindering and urge the inquirer to make confession and forsake the sin. Assurance of salvation will usually result. Use Isaiah 55:7; John 8:12; Ps. 32:1-5.

Another cause of lack of assurance is a dependence on one's feelings. Sometimes the person will feel he is saved, at other times not. It is the counsellor's task to induce him to cease looking inward at his feelings, and to rest his confidence on the sure Word of God. Assure him that God's unchanging Word is far more trustworthy than his own fickle feelings. Using John 3:36, call attention to the fact that 'believing' is certainly followed by 'having' eternal life. Romans 8:1 and John 5:24 affirm that for the believer judgment is past.

Eternal life once given cannot be taken away (John 10:28, 29). The Passover incident has often been effectively used to illustrate this. The sprinkled blood *ensured* the safety of those within the house, while the word of the Lord, believed, *assured* them of safety (Exod. 12:1-13).

An old lady, full of joyous confidence in Christ was asked, 'But suppose Christ should let you slip through one of His fingers?'

She replied at once, 'But I *am* one of His fingers.' There is no possibility of a true believer being separated from the love of Christ (Rom. 8:38, 39).

Do not leave the inquirer until he is able to say with assurance, 'I know that I have eternal life.'

Non-Christians

Those concerned or interested
It is a joy to encounter someone who is genuinely anxious to become a Christian, because they so readily embrace the gospel message.

A man came to the door of our Bible College weeping so profusely that a full minute elapsed before he could tell me of his errand.

'Have you a Bible here?' he inquired.

'Certainly. Come in. What is troubling you? Do you know the joy of having your sins forgiven?' I asked.

'No, but that is what I have come about.'

What a joy it was to lead this prepared man to the Saviour, to see the cloud lift from his face. His handkerchief, already saturated with tears of repentance, did service again, but this time for tears of joy.

He lived hundreds of miles away, and had by his own account been under deep conviction of sin for six months as a result of reading literature sent out by the College, so he had made his way there to secure help.

The first thing to do with one in this condition is to assure him of God's willingness and ability to save (Luke 19:10). Next show that God requires repentance, or a sorrow for sin real enough to make him willing to forsake it (Acts 17:30; Luke 13:3; Isa. 55:7). Repentance involves confession, for God cannot forgiven sin until it is acknowledged (1 John 1:9). Then show what Christ had to suffer before God's love could have full sway, and He could righteously forgive men. It is often very effective to have the seeker read Isaiah 53:3-6, using the first person singular instead of plural, e.g. 'Surely he has borne *my* griefs ... He was wounded for *my* transgressions and bruised for *my* iniquities', etc. This will accomplish the dual purpose of convicting of sin and awakening faith in Christ. Endeavour to make the picture as graphic as possible. Once the inquirer has repented and confessed his need, and been shown the cost at which the gift of eternal life was bought, the next step is to indicate that before he can be saved he must not only repent but believe the gospel (Mark 1:15; Acts 16:31).

But what does it mean to believe? It is of the utmost importance that the counsellor be able to show clearly the nature of saving faith, or what is meant in Scripture by 'Believe on the Lord Jesus Christ.' The sin for which men are condemned is – 'Because they believe not on Me' (John 16:9).

In a letter received recently an inquirer said: 'I believe in Christ, but the devils also believe and tremble, and they are not saved.' Here is the counsellor's problem in a nutshell. There are obviously two kinds of belief – one purely mental, the other involving the whole of the moral nature. The purely intellectual opinion that Christ lived and died for men, works no saving change in the heart or life. What, then, is it to believe to the salvation of the soul? It is to so put your confidence in Christ as being what He claimed to be – your Saviour and sin-bearer – that you put yourself absolutely in His hands for salvation.

If I am suffering from a serious disease for which a certain surgeon says he has an unfailing remedy, it is not sufficient that I believe that he can cure me. That is merely an opinion. I do not really believe *until I put my case in his hands.* I do not believe in my banker until I place my money in his keeping. Believing without trusting is not faith.

Perhaps no illustration is more effective than the old story of Blondin, the tight-rope walker. Having walked the tight-rope across Niagara Falls, first alone, and then pushing a wheelbarrow, he then asked a little fellow who had been watching him breathlessly, whether he believed that he could wheel him across the rope in the barrow.

'Of course I do, sir,' replied the lad, 'I saw you do it.'

'All right, jump in.'

'Oh, no, sir, you don't catch me,' was the honest reply. He believed (mentally), but he did not trust.

Another way of presenting this truth is by showing from John 1:12 that believing and receiving are synonymous. 'As many as received Him' – as Saviour and sin-bearer – 'thereby received the right to become children of God.'

The final step is to lead the inquirer to definitely believe in Christ and receive Him as Saviour. Use John 1:11, 12 again, somewhat as follows: 'You have now confessed your sin and need. You believe that when Jesus died He bore the punishment for your sins and that He longs to be your Saviour and Master. Will you now take Him to be such?'

'Yes, I will.'

'Well, what does this verse say you are now?'

'A child of God.'

'And you are really a child of God already?' If the inquirer is not clear on this point, go over the ground again. Do not leave him until the last doubt has been removed.

It is well to emphasise the divine order – the fact, faith, and then feeling.

> Jesus did it – on the Cross
> God says it – in His Word
> I believe it – in my heart

Feeling that you are saved cannot come before you *are* saved, any more than feeling you are well after an illness cannot come until you are well. And as you cannot be saved without believing, faith must precede feeling. As faith must have a fact to rest on, the fact must precede faith. Many inquirers want to feel saved before they believe in Christ, and they make their feelings the test as to whether or not they have believed, thus reversing the divine order. I believe it, not because I feel it, but because God says it and Jesus did it. Make sure that the inquirer is resting not on his own changeful feelings but on God's unchanging Word.

Those who are indifferent

As these probably constitute the majority among non-Christians, the counsellor must know what methods to adopt to arouse them from their indifference. Erroneous doctrine in many pulpits, worldliness in the church, decay of home-life and family religion, erosion of moral standards have all combined to make many consider that Christianity is irrelevant in the space age. It is our task to show that it is eternally relevant. With these, our aim will be twofold.

To produce conviction of sin. Strictly speaking, this is the work of the Holy Spirit. 'When he comes, he will convict the world of guilt in regard to sin and righteousness and judgment' (John 16:8). Since this is so, we must be very dependent on the Holy Spirit in our conversation.

One Scripture that has been used effectively to this end is Romans 14:12, 'So then each of us will give account of himself to God.' It can be used in some such way as this:

After getting the person being counselled to read the verse himself, ask

'Who has to give account to God?'
'Every one of us.'
'Who does that include?'
'Me'
'Who then is to give account?'
'I am.'
'To whom are you to give account?'
'To God.'
'Of what am I to give account?'
'Myself.'
'Read it that way.'
'I shall give account of myself to God.'
'Are you ready to do that?'

By this time indifference is often changing to concern. You can then show that he has only to continue neglecting God's salvation to be lost (Heb. 2:3).

There are other Scriptures that can be used effectively to produce conviction of sin. The greatness of sin is shown by Matthew 22:36-38; Mark 7:21-23; Romans 3:22, 23; 8:7; Galatians 3:10; James 2:10; 1 John 3:14; Revelation 21:8. The consequences of sin are shown in John 3:36; 8:34; Romans 6:23. Then John 3:17-19 reveals that unbelief in Christ is an appalling and damning sin, while Hebrews 10:28, 29 warns of the certain punishment of those who despise the blood of Christ.

To point to the crucified Christ. The objective of our interview is not to induce the inquirer to embrace a certain doctrine, but to help him to enter into a living relationship with the Son of God. Christ must therefore be presented as the only and the sufficient Saviour who has shown by His death on the cross the reality of His love for us sinful men and women. His resurrection from the dead is evidence of God's satisfaction and acceptance of the atonement He thus made for our sins (Rom. 1:4).

A simple acrostic that has been helpful to beginners in the art of winning men is: '*A*ll have sinned' (Rom. 3:23) – this asserts man's condition before God. '*B*ehold the Lamb of God who takes away the sin of the world' (John 1:29) – this leads the inquirer to the saving Christ. '*C*ome to me and I will give you rest' (Matt. 11:28) – this assures him of Christ's willingness to save and keep. Such verses as Isaiah 53:5, 6; John 3:16; 1 Peter 2:24 may be used to press home the love of God.

Those who have real or contentious problems
These may relate to the Bible or its doctrines, or may be based on the inconsistencies of Christians. In addition to this, many will have personal problems which will need to be treated in the light of the circumstances. Another class is those who have been ensnared in some of the cults that

abound. This field is so large, however, that we leave it to books on that subject. The author's book *Cults and Isms* (Marshall Morgan & Scott, London) could be consulted.

Objections relating to the Bible

'The Bible is full of contradictions'
The counsellor should hand his Bible to the objector, and invite him to show some of them. Do not accept a verbal statement, make him show them from the Bible. In most cases he will be unable to do so, and has thus been put on the defensive. This will open the way for the counsellor to call attention to fulfilled prophecies, the marvellous structural and organic unity of the Book, the confirmations of archaeology, etc. (this assumes that he has done his homework in these areas and is able to give a reason for his hope).

From 1 Corinthians 2:14 it can be shown that the reason he cannot understand the Bible is that he lacks the faculty by which this can be done, and needs to be born anew as commanded in John 3:3, 7. Then he will possess the faculty by which spiritual truth can be understood.

'The Bible is impure'
If this objection is valid, how can it be explained that in every age it has been the purest and most holy people who have found the greatest delight in the Scriptures?

It is true that impure incidents are recorded in Scripture, but never once with approval. The Bible is a realistic book that depicts life as it is. The accounts of the wickedness of men and women are a faithful charting of sunken rocks as a warning to travellers on the ocean of life. Everywhere the Bible faithfully reveals the terrible consequences of sin and impurity.

Paul says, 'To the pure all things are pure, but to those who are corrupted and do not believe, nothing is pure' (1 Titus 1:15). This objection is probably the reflection of the objector's own mind.

'No such being as God exists'

It is a striking fact that the Bible nowhere undertakes to prove the existence of God, but everywhere takes it for granted. The Book opens with the plain assertion of God's existence. 'In the beginning God created the heavens and the earth' (Gen. 1:1).

The existence of a watch argues the existence of a watchmaker. The sound of harmonious music argues for the existence of a musician. The existence of a harmoniously running universe, vast in magnitude yet perfect in detail, argues the existence of an infinitely wise and powerful Creator-God – for every effect must have an adequate cause (Rom. 1:19-23; Ps. 8:1, 3; 33:6). We are surrounded by evidences of His existence which can be ignored only by those who are blinded by prejudice, and this is what the Adversary does. 'The god of this age has blinded the minds of unbelievers' (Tit. 4:5). It is the claim of the Bible that this God is fully revealed in Christ (2 Cor. 4:6).

'There is no such place as Hell'

It is noteworthy that the One who has most to say about hell in the Scriptures is none other than the Son of God, who was love incarnate. Hell is not the invention of Milton or Dante. All of us would like to believe that there is no such place as hell, but if such a belief runs counter to the teachings of Christ, the evangelical Christian has no option but to reject it.

Some who deny this unwelcome doctrine play on the words 'death', 'destruction', 'everlasting', 'eternal'. They claim that they can give you the meaning of the words from the original languages and show that they do not mean that there is eternal punishment for the impenitent; but their objective is not to expound God's statements but rather to support their own view.

If we read such solemn statements as John 3:36; Matthew 25:46; Mark 9:43, 44; Revelation 20:10, 15; 21:8, they certainly *appear* to teach, little though we may like it, that there is a future hell for the finally impenitent. In the parable of the Rich Man and Lazarus, whatever else our Lord meant to teach, he certainly taught that there was an impassable gulf between Lazarus and the rich man.

The expressions 'unto the ages of the ages', and 'for ever and ever' taken in their context can reasonably mean only 'eternal'. Christ nowhere suggests any limitation of time for either reward or suffering, nor is there any clear indication that the doom of the impenitent will know any termination. If this is true, as Scripture appears to teach, it will provide us with strong motivation to seek the lost.

'God is too loving to condemn anyone'

Ask the objector from what source he gained this conception of the character of God. Was it not from the Bible? If he believes the Bible in its assurance that God is a loving God, surely to be consistent he must accept also the same Bible's warning of God's wrath against sin. The Bible reveals God not only as loving, but also as just (2 Pet. 3:9). Ask him to compare John 4:8 with Hebrews 12:29. Although God is loving and good, we are warned against abusing His goodness (Rom. 2:4, 5). The purpose of God's goodness is to lead men to repentance. God's love did not prevent His judgment falling on the wicked before the flood (2 Pet. 2:4-6).

'The Bible is not inspired'

First ask the objector what he understands 'inspired' to mean. In many cases the argument will end when you invite him to define his terms. The counsellor himself, however, must have a clear understanding of the term. A H Strong has this useful definition: 'Inspiration is the special divine influence upon the minds of the Scripture writers, in view of which their productions, apart from errors of transcription, and when rightly interpreted, constitute the infallible rule of faith and practice.'

Point out that in any case, his disbelief does not in any way affect the fact (Rom. 3:3, 4). Usually the one who quibbles on this point has read more about the Scriptures than the Bible itself, and a question as to whether he has ever read the Bible through would be disconcerting and would probably end the argument. If he has never done that, he can hardly pose as an authority. In support of the inspiration of Scripture use: 2 Timothy 3:15, 16; 1 Thessalonians 2:13; 2 Peter 1:19-21; Hebrews 4:12.

Objections based on the inconsistencies of Christians

'There are too many hypocrites in the church'
The counsellor, to be honest, must regretfully concede that this is true in measure, but usually this contention is advanced not so much as a *reason* as an *excuse* for not accepting Christ. If this is true, the person who advances it is himself a hypocrite, for he is not true to his convictions since his real reason is not the hypocrisy of others, but his own disinclination. In answer use Romans 14:12 or Matthew 7:1-5.

Again, show that if there are hypocrites or sham Christians, that very assertion assumes that there are genuine ones. I do not throw away all my coins because there happens to be a counterfeit one among them. Even if some Christians are frauds and hypocrites, Christ is no fraud, and it is to Him you are inviting the inquirer. He does not have to answer for the hypocrite, only for himself. See Romans 14:12; John 21:21, 22.

In any case, since he obviously knows how Christians ought to live, let him set the example, for light brings also responsibility (Luke 12:47). If he does not like hypocrites on earth, he should beware lest he spend all eternity with them, for no hypocrites will enter the pearly gates.

'I have been wrongly treated by Christians'
Unfortunately, again, this may very well be true and should not be condoned.

A man once said to his pastor that the reason he would not accept Christ was that he once had been wronged by his partner, a professing Christian.

'That is your real reason?' asked the minister.

'It is.'

'Suppose we put it down in writing,' said the minister, and

drawing out his notebook, wrote: 'The reason why I am not a Christian is that my partner, who claimed to be a Christian, robbed me in a business deal.' Tearing out the leaf, he handed it to the man, saying: 'When you come before the Great White Throne, and God asks you why you have rejected His Son, just hand Him that paper,' and turning away, he left him.

Hardly had he reached home before the door-bell rang, and there stood the man with the paper in his hand.

'I have brought this paper back,' he said. 'I am afraid it would not answer as an excuse to give to God.'

It was not long before that man was rejoicing in Christ. Even if a man has been wronged, that is no reason why he should do a still greater wrong to himself. See John 3:36; 2 Thessalonians 1:7-9.

Personal difficulties and problems

In the course of engaging in personal evangelism, one will come in contact with many people who are not antagonistic and are quite sincere. They are sheltering behind excuses for not becoming a Christian that seem valid to them, but will not stand up to close scrutiny.

'I am doing my best'
This is a common contention, but Scripture maintains that man's best is not acceptable to God (Isa. 64:6). Paul made it clear that 'A man is not justified by observing the law [doing one's best] but by faith in Jesus Christ' (Gal. 2:16). If our own works and attainments are to form the ground of our acceptance, then only perfect holiness in thought, word and deed can satisfy an ethically perfect God. Would the inquirer measure up to this standard?

'I am not very bad'
This may be true according to his own standards of goodness, but how does he measure up to God's standard, for it is to Him he must give account (Rom. 3:10, 23). Press these Scriptures home and show that while he may consider

himself acceptable in God's sight he is a sinful man. It may be necessary to show what sin really is in relation to God. If he admits that he has sinned and is therefore a sinner, show that it is the *fact* of his sin, not the *magnitude* of it, which is in question. A chain mooring a ship does not need to be broken in every link to set the ship adrift; one broken link is enough (James 2:10). Jesus indicated that the greatest, the finally damning sin is not to believe on Him (John 16:9).

'*I go to church*' or '*I have been baptised or confirmed*'

These things are very right and important in their place, but they do not remove the need to be born again (John 3:3, 7). Many have been taught to think that these constitute man's whole duty to God, and that when the final day comes all will be well with them.

An alien who put on a British or American uniform without enlisting in the army would be looked on as a spy, and shot. No one but a loyal soldier has a right to wear it. Only those who have been born into the family of God through the new birth are entitled to wear Christ's uniform. While every true Christian should be baptised and join the fellowship of a church, the mere doing of these things works no saving change. Only faith in Christ can do this.

'*I have always believed in Christ*'

There are undoubtedly cases where people who give every evidence of being true Christians cannot remember a time when they did not believe in and trust Christ. But this statement usually comes from someone who really means that *he believes certain facts and doctrines about Christ.* There is a big difference between intellectually accepting the historical fact that Christ died on the cross for our sins, and definitely trusting Him alone for salvation. It would clarify the issue to ask, 'Then since you have always believed in Christ, do you possess eternal life?' Usually the answer will be a hesitating consent or a direct negative. The way will then be open to explain what believing in Christ means.

'*I cannot believe*'

When a person who seems sincere makes this excuse, there is often a moral cause behind it. God never commands anyone to do what they cannot do, so when He commands all men everywhere to repent and believe the gospel, all can believe if there is no hindering obstacle to belief. Remove the hindrance, and belief will be automatic. By questioning, discover if there is some sin he is unwilling to part with. Use Isaiah 55:7! God says he *can* believe (John 1:12), and *must* believe (Heb. 11:6). Failure to believe inevitably incurs judgment (John 3:18).

Another effective method is to ask, 'Whom is it you cannot believe? Can you not believe God who showed His loving concern for you by giving His Son to die for you?' 'Yes, I can believe God, but I can't trust myself'. 'You are not asked to. You are asked to believe in Christ. "Believe in the Lord Jesus and you will be saved"' (Acts 16:31).

'*I have tried before and failed*'

This is often a very genuine and distressed confession, and the inquirer is reluctant to 'try again', in case he might fail. Evidently he has conceived the Christian life to be one of self-effort. We all want to effect our own salvation, but this attitude is probably at the root of his failure. Salvation does not come by *trying* to do one's best, but by *trusting* Him who achieved our salvation on the cross. It is a gift to be accepted, not a reward to be earned (Rom. 6:23).

Some leading questions may be asked to diagnose his condition. 'Did you really trust Christ and commit your whole life to Him for salvation?' 'Have you confessed Him as Lord and Saviour before men?' (Rom. 10:9, 10; Matt. 10:32, 33). In many cases the answer will be negative, and you have discovered one possible cause of failure.

'Did you read the Scriptures and pray daily?' (1 Pet. 2:2; 1 Thess. 5:17). 'Did you trust Christ's promise to keep you from falling?' (2 Cor. 12:9; Jude 24). 'Have you witnessed for Christ?'

If your questions leave a doubt as to his conversion, lead

him to faith in Christ, and show His ability to keep those who put their trust in Him.

'I am too weak'
The prescription for this person is to direct his attention away from himself and his very real weakness to the Christ who is strong. 'It is not a question of your undoubted weakness but of Christ's almighty power' (Heb. 7:25). God is willing to strengthen the weakest believer (2 Cor. 9:10; Isa. 40:29-31). No one is too weak to trust Christ. The keeping power is His, not ours (Jude 24; 1 Pet. 1:5; 1 Tim. 1:12; John 10:28, 29). There will be temptations, but for every temptation there is a built-in way to escape provided (1 Cor. 10:13). When God begins a work in a life, He finishes it (Phil. 1:6).

'I am too wicked'
Do not try to minimise the sinfulness which the inquirer has admitted. Tell him that if we could see ourselves as God sees us, we would realise that we are a great deal more sinful than we thought. But Christ said that He did not come to call the righteous, but the wicked to repentance (Luke 19:10). Paul claims in 1 Timothy 1:15 that he was the foremost of sinners, yet Christ saved him, so there is hope for all others (see Isa. 1:18; Heb. 7:25; 1 John 1:7).

'I've done no one any harm'
One could laughingly remark that this is a very negative qualification for acceptance with God. It would not reflect much credit on him if he had done harm to others. Surely he has a higher aim in life than not doing harm to others. God requires not mere negative harmlessness but positive holiness and this can come only through becoming a child of God through faith in Christ (John 1:12). Ask if he has attained to God's standard of holiness (Rom. 3:23; Matt. 5:20).

'I see no harm in the innocent pleasures of the world'
There are of course many innocent pleasures that we can

enjoy without any sense of guilt. But the focal point in this excuse is in our definition of 'world'. In biblical usage, the term 'world', in an ethical sense, conveys the idea of human society so organised as to exclude God. That is why James says that 'friendship with the world is hatred towards God. Anyone who chooses to be a friend of the world becomes an enemy of God' (James 4:4). That does not sound too innocent! Pleasures of the world in which there is no place for God and Christ are not innocent. There is a barb concealed in them all.

The counsellor should not be entirely negative, but show the pure and unalloyed joy that the Christian experiences – and without any hangover. Testimony to this may be in order.

'There is too much to give up if I accept Christ'

The cost of Christian discipleship should not be played down, for there is a cost which Jesus did not fail to emphasise (Luke 14:26-28, 33). The young ruler who would not face the cost of following Christ went away sorrowful. Jesus said that the loss of everything would be better than losing one's own soul (Mark 8:36).

But God requires us to give up only those things which are sinful and are against our own highest interests (Psalm 84:11; Rom. 8:32).

'I can't give up my sins'

While being sympathetic to his plight if the person being counselled is sincere, do not compromise with the necessity of having done with his sins which obviously have him in their grasp. Show him, however, that Christ can strengthen him and enable him to break with sin (Phil. 4:13). An unwillingness to turn from his sin and accept Christ will involve him in eternal loss (Rom. 6:23; Gal. 6:7, 8; Rev. 21:8). If he will trust Christ for salvation, he will become a new person with new desires (2 Cor. 5:17). John 8:36 holds out an alluring prospect. Show from Romans 6:12-14 how victory over sin is possible to the Christian.

'I am not ready to come yet'

Many people really desire and intend to become Christians, but they allow the devil to delude them into postponing their commitment to Christ.

A minister determined to preach on 'Now is the accepted time, now is the day of salvation.' While in his study thinking, he fell asleep and dreamed that he was carried into hell and set down in the midst of a conclave of lost spirits. They were assembled to devise means whereby they might damn the souls of men.

One rose and said: 'I will go to earth and tell men the Bible is a fable.'

'No, that would not do.'

Another said: 'Let me go. I will tell men that there is no God, no Saviour, no heaven, no hell.'

'No, that will not do, we cannot make them believe *that*.'

Suddenly one arose and with a wise look suggested: 'I will tell men there is a God, a Saviour, a heaven, yes and a hell, too – but I will tell them there is no hurry; tomorrow will do, it will be the same as today.' And they sent him. This was the devil's trump card. It is still one of his most successful ploys.

I was preaching at a seaside resort some years ago. In the service was a young man who was very fond of yachting. He was moved by the message, but he went out at the close. His Bible Class leader induced him to return and speak to me, but he was reluctant to make any commitment.

I said to him, 'Supposing you were some miles from shore and your yacht overturned in a squall, how would you stand with God?'

'Oh,' he responded, 'I'm too good a yachtsman for that to happen!'

Two or three weeks later he was yachting with a friend. When three miles from shore, a storm arose and the yacht overturned and they were unable to right it. His friend was the stronger swimmer, so he struck out for the shore to obtain help. They returned only to find that the young man had been swept into the sea.

God's acceptable time is *now* (2 Cor. 6:2; Acts 17:30). Life is so uncertain that delay is always dangerous. It can be pointed out that we are exhorted to 'seek the Lord, while He may be found' (Isa. 55:6). The implication is that He will not always be at our beck and call (see Prov. 29:1; Luke 12:19, 20; Matt. 24:44; John 7:33, 34).

'I wish to be a Christian, but I don't know how'

It will be an unmixed joy to lead this prepared heart along the familiar steps to faith in Christ. First step, repent of your sin (Psa. 51:3, 4). Second step, believe, place your trust in the Christ who died for your sins (Acts 16:31; John 1:12). Third step, confess Christ as your Saviour to someone (Rom. 10:9, 10; Matt. 10:32, 33) and continue to confess Him.

'I have sought to find Christ, but have not found Him'

If this is indeed so, the reason is in the seeker and not in God. God assures us, 'You will seek me and find me *when you seek me with all your heart*' (Jer. 29:13). This is the crux of the problem. Has there been such a wholehearted search as involved repentance and the forsaking of sin? Most probably there has been insincerity, not seeking with the whole heart.

'I am afraid of persecution'

In this century in which there have been more martyrs for Christ than in any other period in church history, this can be a very genuine reservation in some lands.

Our Lord never promised His followers exemption from persecution. Indeed, He affirmed that in the world we would have tribulation. Jesus dealt with this fear in Luke 12:4, 5; see also Isaiah 51:7, 8; Proverbs 29:25. The early Christians had such joy in Christ that they rejoiced in suffering persecution for His sake (Acts 5:41). Jesus included such persecution in His beatitudes (Matt. 5:10, 11). Think of the promised reward (2 Tim. 2:12; Rom. 8:18).

'I guess I'll make it to heaven all right'

He will if he comes the right way, and the only way is through Christ (John 14:6; 1 Tim. 2:5; Acts 4:12). Unless his sins are cleansed and removed through faith in the atoning Christ, he cannot hope to enter heaven, for nothing impure will ever enter into that holy and happy place (1 Cor. 6:9,10; Rev. 21:27).

'I will lose my friends'

The truth is that he will gain far more friends than he will lose, for he will become a member of the whole family of God. But in any case, if his friends are such that they would hinder him from getting right with God and experiencing the joy of salvation, he would be better without them (Ps. 1:1, 2).

God promises blessing on those who renounce worldly friendships for His sake. In place of godless friends, God will give first His own friendship (1 John 1:3), and then that of fellow-Christians who share the same tastes and ideals.

'The Christian life sounds too difficult'

Satan would like seekers after God to believe that this is so, but in fact it is the way of transgressors that is hard (Prov. 13:5; Isa. 14:3). On the other hand, Jesus affirms that His yoke is easy and His burden light (Matt. 11:30).

The Christian life as Peter depicts it and millions of Christians have proved it, has its disciplines and involves enduring hardship like a good soldier of Jesus Christ, but the compensations are so immeasurably greater that the Christian is able to count it all joy (James 1:2).

As Peter describes the Christian life it does not sound too exacting and forbidding: 'Without having seen him, you love him; though you do not now see him, you believe in him and rejoice with unutterable and exalted joy' (1 Pet. 1:8).

'I do not feel saved'

Remind the inquirer that it is through *believing* in Christ that we are saved, and become children of God, and not by any special feeling. It is 'by grace we are saved, *through faith',* not through feeling (Eph. 2:8). Salvation comes through receiving, rather than through feeling (John 1:12; Rom. 6:23). When I receive the gift of salvation, the appropriate emotion will follow. Ask if he knows of one Scripture that says he must feel saved in order to be saved. Feeling follows faith, it does not precede it.

'I have committed the unpardonable sin'
First be sure yourself as to the nature of the unpardonable
sin. Read Matthew 12:31, 32 in its context, where it is plain
that this sin consists in deliberately attributing to the devil
the work which is known to have been wrought by the Holy
Spirit. Ask the inquirer if he has done this. It is evident that
one who is anxious about his soul cannot have committed
this sin, since that anxiety is the direct result of the work of
the Holy Spirit. Having shown what the sin is, hold the
inquirer to John 6:37, with its unconditional promise that
anyone, however good or bad, who comes to Christ, will
never be driven away. Do not give up until he 'comes' to
Christ.

7

An Illustration and an Example

I make myself a slave to everyone, to win as many as possible
(1 Cor. 9:19)

The word 'win', used so frequently in connection with our theme, may legitimately be applied to the captivating of human affections. The figure of the bridegroom wooing and winning his bride is frequently elevated to the spiritual realm in Scripture. Believers are referred to as the Bride of Christ. Paul refers to them as being 'married to another' (Rom. 7:4). The soul-winner can therefore be regarded as one whose task is to captivate the affections of men and attach them to Christ.

A typical illustration

No more beautiful illustration of the work of the winner of men can be found in the Scriptures than the winning of Rebekah as a bride for Isaac as recorded in Genesis 24.

Abraham delegated to his trusted steward the responsible task of securing a bride for his son, first giving him specific instructions. Eliezer was eminently fitted for the task. He was *born in Abraham's house*, and thus had an intimate knowledge of his master and his plans for his son. He who would win people to Christ, too, must through intimate fellowship with the Father, enter into His purposes for His only Son.

Eliezer had been heir to Abraham's great wealth until Isaac was born, but now his whole life was *unreservedly yielded to the service of the one who superseded him* (cf.

Gen. 15:2-4; 24:36 with John 3:29, 30). He was totally free of envy.

With reference to his mission it should be noted that Abraham *revealed to him his secret purpose* – to obtain a suitable wife for his son. God has similarly shared with us His secret purpose for His Son (Acts 15:14).

Eliezer *received definite instructions* where to go and where not to go. He was not bound to approach every young woman whom he met. Even so we are not called upon to speak to every person who crosses our path, but only those to whom the Holy Spirit directs us. Willingness to present Christ to anyone, anywhere will, if we have an attentive ear for the promptings of the Spirit, deliver us from bondage and bring us into a joyous liberty in this work.

He was deprived of all honour, but was also freed from all responsibility. The responsibility for results is not ours. Our responsibility extends only to faithfully presenting God's message and saturating it with prayer.

Much can be learned from the eager yet prudent way in which Eliezer fulfilled his mission.

He did not underestimate the difficulty of persuading a young woman to go with him, a stranger, to be the bride of a man whom she had never seen. He knew the wealth and glory that awaited the bride of Isaac, but she did not share that knowledge. The Christian worker knows the unsearchable riches of Christ, but as he has nothing tangible with which to appeal to the senses of his 'prospect', he sometimes fears that his Master will be rejected. It is just here that he, as did Eliezer, must rely on the ministry of the Angel.

He proposed an unacceptable expedient – to take Issac with him. Abraham rejected the proposal. Isaac had to be offered to the woman in a verbal message by the chosen messenger. Sometimes the bare Word of God unaccompanied by tangible evidence seems to us painfully inadequate to lure a person away from the world to Christ. Yet when this 'sword' is wielded in the power of the Spirit, it is 'living and active'. It is still true that 'faith comes by hearing, and hearing by the Word of God'.

His dependence on the Angel did not cut the nerve of his

own endeavours. He prayed and acted as though all depended on him. He knew that God had chosen a bride for Isaac, but he still prayed that he might be directed to the one of God's choice, and then put himself in the way of the Lord's leading. A pilot cannot guide a ship while it is moored to the wharf, but once the shore lines are cast off the ship can be steered to its destination. So when we take an initial step of faith, the Holy Spirit can guide us.

He subordinated his own comforts and interests to those of his master. He would not so much as satisfy his hunger until he had unburdened his heart. He spoke, not of himself, but of 'my master' (vv. 12, 27, 34).

His method of approach was as suited to the success of his mission as was his attitude.

He prayed before he made the proposal, and during the negotiations. Nor did he forget to lift his heart in praise as he saw the plan unfolding.

He delivered his message clearly and convincingly. His master had one wonderful son to whom he had given all his wealth. He desired a bride for his son from his own family line. Rebekah was the bride God had chosen, as the events that had transpired indicated. Would she consent?

'The Father loves the Son,' said our Lord, 'and has given all things into his hands.' The task of the worker is to present clearly and winsomely the facts of the gospel, with a view to inducing men and women to accept the Son.

Eliezer used no undue pressure, although he was desperately anxious that the answer should be 'Yes.' That was the responsibility of the Angel.

There is always a thrilling pause when a person is brought to the point of receiving Christ as Saviour, but it is the role of the Holy Spirit to draw that person to say 'Yes' to Christ. The wise counsellor will never force a decision, although he will make clear the urgency of making a decision. Eliezer waited a whole night to give Rebekah time to reflect on the offer. When she answered, 'I will go,' he was well rewarded for an anxious night.

He expected swift success. Less than a day had elapsed before the bride was on her way to meet Isaac. But she met with opposition from her family. Her mother and brother wanted her to stay at least ten days. Eager Eliezer would not hear of it. 'Do not delay me,' he objected. Satan is the prince of delays, but a human soul is too precious to win and nearly lose again. Not all conversions are sudden, but church history reveals that very many have been so.

Our last glimpse of Eliezer is in communion with his loved master. He was able to report 'Mission fulfilled!' He presents the bride, tells how he had been prospered, and fades out of the picture, leaving Isaac alone with Rebekah. When we meet with success in our mission, let us emulate his self-effacement.

A perfect example

Have you ever pondered the fact that the greater part of the harvest of our Lord's ministry was hand-gathered fruit? Seven of the eleven apostles, and probably the other four as well, were won by individual appeal. In the Gospels of Matthew and John at least *sixteen private interviews* are recorded for our instruction. This should suffice to convince us that the Master considered personal soul-winning of primary importance. In this, as in everything else, He is a shining example.

Christ was a unique winner of men. Knowing as He did what was in man (John 2:25), knowing the workings of the human mind which He had fashioned, His methods in treating various people are text-book models for us. In His dealing with human hearts He never transgressed a psychological law. Let us note some of the lessons we can learn from His methods with individuals.

He was not class-conscious. He had conversations with the ruling class, e.g. Nicodemus and the young ruler. He conversed with business men, men of the middle class, e.g. Zaccheus. But He did not neglect the proletariat and outcasts, e.g. the woman of Samaria. To each class He manifested the same loving concern.

His approach was always tactful. Frequently He commenced a conversation by introducing a point of common interest, from which He could lead the conversation to spiritual realities. His question to the leper, 'Do you want to be made whole?' was a matter of burning interest to the sufferer. He found common ground with Nicodemus in his interest in the Kingdom of God. He told Peter the fisherman that He would make him a fisher of men. He led the conversation with the Samaritan woman from well-water to living water.

He commended people rather than condemned them. Honest commendation is one of the quickest ways to the human heart. On one occasion I was eating lunch with a friend who was a zealous personal evangelist. Suddenly he rose from the table and went up to an old man whom I thought must be a friend of his. When he returned to his seat, I asked who the man was.

My friend had never seen him before, but as the old man came in he noticed that he had an old-fashioned gold watch chain from which hung a gold medal. He immediately saw a chance to speak for His Lord. He enquired how the medal had been won, and the man was only too ready to tell his story. This opened the way for a spiritual conversation. Such a possibility never occurred to my mind.

Our Lord doubtless perceived many defects in the character of Nathanael, but He opened his interview by commending him for his freedom from guile. Nothing will more quickly dissipate prejudice than this approach. A judgmental attitude tends to alienate and close the way to further advances.

He constantly illustrated His talks with parables and illustrations drawn from contemporary life, and which were within the range of knowledge of his hearers. One of the Evangelists wrote 'He did not say anything to them without using a parable' (Matt. 13:34). We would be wise to follow His example.

He refused to be drawn into profitless argument. When faced with an argumentative lawyer who demanded an answer to his quibbling question 'Who is my neighbour?', the Lord so completely disarmed him with the parable of the

Good Samaritan, that he had no further argument to present. Jesus refused to be sidetracked from the main issue. Paul gave the same advice to Timothy (2 Tim. 2:23).

Jesus wept and prayed over lost men and women, believing that as the psalmist said, unless He sowed in tears, He would not reap with joy (126:4, 6).

He never failed to make a personal application of His teachings as in the case of the Samaritan woman who testified, 'Come, see a man who told me all that I ever did' (John 4:29). To Nicodemus He said, 'You must be born anew'.

In His interview with the Samaritan woman (John 4), we see a representative illustration of His method. She was an adulteress who had not grown shameless, for she went to draw water when no one was about. She was proud of her descent, and was a religious formalist. She had a slick tongue and was quick to turn serious things into jests.

In order to win her, Jesus went out of his way, and by-passed conventional standards. The rabbinic law said: 'Let no man talk with a woman on the street; no, not with his own wife.' But it should be noted that He acted with discretion, and arranged to meet her not at dusk, but at midday. Nor did He interview her in the presence of others. Instead of scolding or reproaching her, He asked a favour. He also ignored racial barriers.

He taught her spiritual truth through familiar metaphor. He refused to be diverted from His objective, and after parrying her questions, ceased to beat about the bush and came to close quarters (v. 16). But He did not evade the point she had raised (vv. 20-22).

It is an interesting example of the deviousness of the human heart to notice the barriers the woman erected in self-defence: the sex barrier (v. 9); the racial barrier (v. 9); the religious barrier (vv. 19, 20). But the Lord ruthlessly demolished them all and exposed the corruption of her heart to her own gaze. She tried in every way possible to evade the issue, but the Master held her to it.

She appealed to her ancestry, told a half-truth in a fruitless endeavour to conceal her guilt, concurred in what He said, and sought to flatter Him. But every time He brought her back to face her own guilt and need.

The culmination of this remarkable interview is reached in verses 25 and 26, when Jesus revealed Himself as the Messiah. 'The woman said to him, "I know the Messiah is coming . . ." Jesus said to her, "I who speak to you am he"'. The ultimate objective of all evangelism had been reached.

8

Working Among the Cults

One of the most remarkable characteristics of the contemporary religious scene is the 'cult explosion', for no other term can adequately describe the proliferation of heresies and cults in the last fifty years. By a cult we mean, to use Webster's definition, 'any religion regarded as unorthodox or even spurious.'

It would be easy to ignore them, or to feel that their adherents are so dogmatic or besotted in their views that there is little hope of winning them to true faith in Christ. While it is true that this is one of the most difficult fields for personal evangelism, that does not absolve us from our responsibility to witness to them. They are all included in Paul's comprehensive statement: 'I feel myself under a sort of universal obligation, I owe something to all men, from cultured Greek to ignorant savage' (Rom. 1:14, Phillips).

In engaging in this work, we may learn much from the cults themselves. Gerald E Richter writes in this connection: 'Some phases of the cults' operations might well be emulated by their non-productive critics. They believe strongly in what they profess. They sacrifice of their slender means to a far greater extent than the more prosperous members of more orthodox faiths. They publish literature expounding their views literally by the ton, and devote hours, days, weeks of gratuitous service in its circulation that others may share with them the satisfying experiences into which they have entered. How different are the "activities" of the more respected churches!'

While the church cannot be charged with the full responsibility for the phenomenal growth of these new cults, she is by no means free from blame. It has been said, and with justification, that 'the cults are the unpaid bills of the church.' All too many have been ensnared because of a lack of teaching of the basic tenets of the Christian faith or because they have found more warmth of fellowship in the new group. But whatever the reason for their defection, we have responsibility to bring them face to face with the truth.

A study of many of these modern cults reveals not only a substantial identity with some of the heresies that distressed the early church, but also a striking, almost monotonous similarity in their denials of the great essentials of the Christian faith.

In order to be able to prescribe the appropriate remedy, we must endeavour to sympathetically understand the background of those we are seeking to help.

Many, especially among the younger generation, are disillusioned with the Establishment, and with the blatant materialism of our age. Some have turned to the protest movements, some to drugs and some to the appealing religious substitutes offered by the new cults.

Then, too, we are constantly being bombarded by predictions of doom as a result of nuclear warfare, the pollution crisis, the population explosion, the computer monster. With such a frightening prospect, many who have not had the true Christian alternative presented to them fall for the false.

The breakdown of the family and the disintegration of society have created an entirely new grouping of solo parents, delinquent children and unmarried people living together. To these 'lost' people some of the cults make a strong appeal.

One other factor is the appeal of the occult. People are becoming increasingly fascinated by the occult and esoteric religions. In its June 19, 1972 issue, *Time* magazine had this to say:

> A wave of fascination with the occult is noticeable throughout the country. It first became apparent a few years ago in the astrology boom, which continues. But today it extends all the way from Satanism and witchcraft to the edges of science. Major publishers have issued dozens of hard-cover books on the occult and the related field of parapsychology in the past

year ... A growing number of colleges across the USA are offering courses on aspects of the occult.

There are certain things that we should bear in mind in our approach to adherents of a cult. We are not dealing with irreligious people, but rather with those who are fanatically religious. Usually they have rejected what they consider to be historic Christianity and firmly believe that they have at last found the truth. In many cases they are convinced of the superiority of their doctrines which they claim have been received by special revelation. They can point to the unity of their group as compared with the all too evident divisions in the church. Further, many of them have suffered deeply for their beliefs and will not be easily prised away from them.

How should we approach adherents of cults?

It need hardly be said that we should approach these people in a spirit of genuine love and not of hostility. Anthony Hoekema tells of a woman, formerly a Jehovah's Witness, who reported that while a Witness she encountered three types of responses. 'Some slammed the door in her face. These people made her feel good, since their action was construed to be persecution for the sake of her faith. A second group argued heatedly and belligerently. These only strengthened her convictions, since she had ready answers for their arguments. A third group gave her a personal testimony of their faith in Christ. These, so she said, made the most lasting impression on her. When she went to bed at night, she would think about these people and reflect on what they had said.'

If you are *not really well-grounded in the Scriptures* and not yet experienced in presenting the gospel to those who are opposed, you would probably be wise to confine your efforts to simply giving your testimony to your faith in Christ. Wait until you are better equipped before trying to meet and answer the arguments of those who are usually very well indoctrinated in their own particular teachings. Don't try to argue with them about their errors, but bear positive testimony to the truth as you have experienced it, and of the assurance and satisfaction it has brought to you.

We are exhorted, however: 'Always be prepared to give an answer to everyone who asks you to give the reason for the hope that you have' (1 Peter 3:15). This will mean that you should study the Scriptures with this end in view. If we are going to be effective in this type of evangelism, we must (a) be familiar with the great doctrines of the Christian faith, and (b) learn the special teaching of the religious group involved.

In most of these new religions, one or all of the following errors will be involved:

Faulty or inadequate teachings about Christ. John states that the man who denies that Jesus is the Christ (Messiah) is the antichrist (1 John 2:22). He also says that 'This is how you can recognise the Spirit of God: Every spirit that acknowledges that *Jesus Christ is come in the flesh* is from God, but every spirit that does not acknowledge Jesus is not of God' (1 John 4:2). So the first question to ask is, 'What do they teach about Christ?'

A considerable number of these new religions *deny the Trinity of the Godhead* and that there is only one God who eternally exists and manifests Himself to us in three Persons – Father, Son and Holy Spirit. So the question must be asked, 'What do they teach about the Trinity?' (Matt. 28:19; 3:17-19; Rom. 8:9-11).

Yet other cults ignore, belittle or *deny the atoning death of Christ* as a substitutionary sacrifice on our behalf (1 Cor. 5:21; 15:3; Heb. 9:22). It is not sufficient to view His death as merely a heroic example.

Most of these cults advocate some system of self-salvation. The doctrine of *justification by faith in Christ alone* is rejected, as also is the concept that Christ is the *only* way to God, the *only* door into the Kingdom (Rom. 4:2-5; 5:1; 6:23; John 14:6; 10:9; Acts 4:12).

As there are many cults that do not recognise the validity and authority of the Bible, you should be sure of your own position on this point. For a young Christian a book like *Can I Trust the Bible* by Howard Vos (Moody Press) would give valuable instruction. In our use of Scripture, however, we should remember that 'the Word of God is living and active' (Heb. 4:12) even though the person to whom we are speaking does not accept its authority. The Bible is self-authenticating.

The purely intellectual approach to the cultist may often prove ineffective, because few people are motivated purely by reason. We are motivated by a great variety of considerations. They may be seeking fellowship and security rather than the solution of intellectual problems, for man is heart as well as head.

Some are perplexed as to the meaning of 2 John 10 and 11: 'If anyone comes to you and does not bring this teaching, do not take him into your house, or welcome him.' John is here referring to teachers of false doctrine who come not as casual visitors but as official teachers. To them we are not to extend an official welcome. But this does not mean that we may not entertain someone who holds false views, and endeavour to show him the true way of salvation. It may possibly be that the 'house' John was referring to was not a private home, but the house in which many churches of that day met for worship.

As to our attitude to cultists whom we seek to win for Christ, these cautions may be in order:

1. Approach the task with genuine humility and dependence on the Holy Spirit. It is a task beyond mere human wisdom.

2. Do not approach the individual in a judgmental spirit but with genuine love. When Jesus saw such people 'He was moved with compassion.'

3. In most cults there are elements of truth. Do not be afraid to acknowledge this.

4. Do not impute unworthy motives. They may in fact be as sincere as you are, although wrong.

5. Never quote a text unless you are sure of its context. Proof-texts can sometimes backfire.

6. Finally, in approaching a cultist, 'our concern should be

to approach him as a total person – that is, not just as someone whose doctrines need to be refuted, but as someone we love, about whom we are concerned in the totality of his life' (A Hoekema).

> Stir me, oh stir me, Lord! Thy heart was stirred
>   By love's intensest fire, till Thou didst give
> Thine only Son, Thy best beloved One,
>   E'en to the dreadful cross, that I might live;
> Stir me to give myself so back to Thee
>   That Thou canst give Thyself again through me.

9

Children's Evangelism

This subject merits a whole book, but a few suggestions are included. As the author received Christ and eternal life at the age of eight, and his wife similarly at the age of six, he had no problems about the possibility of child conversion. Jesus spoke of 'little ones that believe in me' (Matt. 18:6). As the Master soul-winner said, 'Let the little children come to me and do not hinder them,' his followers must do the same, 'for the Kingdom of heaven belongs to such as these' (Matt. 19:14). Dr Reuben A Torrey maintained that no other form of Christian work brings such immediate, such large, and such lasting results as work for the conversion of children. There is reason to believe that capacity for believing lies more in the child than in the adult (Matt. 18:6). Children have fewer prejudices to overcome than adults.

Parents, of course, have primary responsibility for the religious training of the child, and this should not be largely delegated to others, as is too often the case. The parent who neglects this privilege not only fails in his duty, but unwittingly robs himself of one of the highest joys of life. Why should the winning of one's own child be left to a stranger?

The following suggestions have been made for successful work among children.

There must be a genuine belief in the child's need, and the possibility of his salvation. We believe, of course, in the salvation of children who have not reached the years of moral accountability. But the child, no less than the adult, is 'dead in trespasses and sins' and needs and is capable of receiving salvation. While we believe that children are covered by the atoning sacrifice of Christ until they reach the age of accountability, that does not mean that they cannot truly repent of sin and exercise faith in Christ. History is on the side of child conversion.

There should be a clear understanding of one's mission, not to instruct or amuse only, but to lead the child in a natural and simple way to receive the Lord into his heart and to become His disciple. The child has less problem in believing than the adult.

There must be reliance on the Spirit's conviction and illumination as much with children as with adults.

There must be adaptation to the capacity of the child. We need our best and most industrious studies and to employ the most suitable methods in presenting the truth to children. Today there is an abundance of material available for this purpose.

We must present truth in the child's language. There is no need to use baby talk, but it should be simple, vivid and easy to understand.

We should not expect too much of children, a tendency to which most of us are prone. It is right for a child to have childish ways and we should not try to get them to abandon them. A child who acts like an adult is anything but desirable. They should be allowed to mature at their own pace.

We will have need of patience. If we recall our own childhood and our own immaturity and stumblings, we will more easily bear with the disappointments that child evangelism sometimes brings.

Especial wisdom and restraint should be exercised in making an evangelistic appeal to children, because it is very easy to get the whole class or audience to respond. There may be times when a very low-key appeal could be made, but this should be done sparingly. It is a great mistake to make appeals frequently for children easily become accustomed and hardened to them, and as a result may become more difficult to reach in later life.

One evangelist invites children present at his meetings, if they desire to receive Christ as Saviour, to go home, and write their name in John 3:16 instead of 'the world' and 'whosoever', and post it to him, or hand it to him the next day. This avoids the use of undue pressure and the danger of children responding because others are doing so.

It is encouraging to remember that D L Moody was converted at fourteen years of age, Fanny Crosby at eleven, Jonathan Edwards at seven, Isaac Watts at nine. The author was converted at eight. Almost ninety per cent of Christians are converted before they reach eighteen.

The Scripture Union has very useful junior daily reading notes specially adapted to children, and the Child Evangelism Fellowship also has valuable aids.

10

Tract Evangelism

This form of evangelism is not so popular as it was some years ago, but it still has a useful ministry.

The fact that attractive tracts and leaflets are still used so widely by various cults should alert us to the fact that this form of evangelism can still be fruitfully employed. Many who would never enter a church will read an attractive and pleasantly offered tract.

The following suggestions could make this approach more effective:

Use only well-written and attractively printed tracts. There are tract societies that aim at producing masses of tracts, but these are sometimes poorly printed on poor paper and are not a good advertisement for the gospel.

Know your tracts. Don't distribute tracts you have not read. No one tract will meet all needs so discretion should be used in selection. People are likely to be interested in tracts that speak to their own situation, so they should be contemporary.

Always be cheerful and courteous as you approach a prospect. An unsmiling, dour face will not attract anyone to read your tract. Make some relevant and cheerful remark that will open the way for a conversation. The courteous distributor will seldom be rebuffed.

If you are rebuffed, you are presented with an opportunity to manifest the love of Christ. Our attitude to a rebuff can be a testimony to Christ.

Follow up the opening the giving of the tract has made, and explain the plan of salvation.

Broadcast distribution can be made from house to house, in the street if permissible, in hospitals, etc. A great proportion of tracts so distributed will be wasted, but some of the seed sown will bear fruit.

As an encouragement to those who engage in this form of evangelism and a challenge to those who do not, the story of the chain of blessing which followed one tract is given. This tract, written by Dr Richard Gibbs, was handed by a pedlar to Richard Baxter, whose *Call to the Unconverted* fell into the hands of Philip Doddridge, the great preacher and hymn-writer. He wrote *The Rise and Progress of Religion*, by means of which William Wilberforce, the emancipator of slaves, was converted. He in turn wrote *Practical Christianity*, which fired the heart of Leigh Richmond, who in turn wrote *The Dairyman's Daughter*, of which, before 1848, four million copies were circulated in fifty languages. Wilberforce's book also fell into the hands of Thomas Chalmers, and was the means of bringing him out into the light of the Gospel, and all Scotland rang with his mighty eloquence.

The potential for blessing of a good tract should never be underestimated.

11

The Consecrated Pen

Who can estimate the blessing that has flowed, the lives that have been changed through a consecrated pen? Have you ever thought of your pen as an instrument of evangelism?

Here is a form of service that is open to the timid person who finds it difficult to summon up courage to talk to someone about Christ face to face. Let such a person pray, 'Lord, consecrate my pen to Your use' and then use it for Him.

I was travelling in Asia with Fred Mitchell, the British Director of the China Inland Mission. We separated at Singapore as he flew on to London. His plane exploded as it left Calcutta and all aboard lost their lives.

This was a terrible blow to his widow, who was in delicate health. When she had recovered somewhat from the shock, she began to think how this traumatic experience could be used for God's glory. Then it occurred to her, 'You are only one of thousands who have been widowed. Why not share your experience of God's salvation and comfort with other widows?' In this simple way a fruitful ministry opened up to one who consecrated her pen to God's service.

Dr H Clay Trumbull, one of the greatest personal evangelists of his day, was converted through a letter written to him by a college mate who had not the courage to speak to him personally.

The same fruitful avenue of service is open to the invalid or to the mother whose children are away from home. The letter will probably be read and re-read, whereas a spoken word might be forgotten.

In engaging in letter-evangelism, pray before and after writing each letter, asking wisdom to express the truth in a winsome manner.

Letters should be simple, clear and sympathetically written. One's own testimony would often be appropriate to include. Paul gave his testimony three times as recorded in the Acts. Do not quote too many Scriptures.

Having presented the plan of salvation, urge the recipient to definitely accept Christ as Saviour without delay. An appropriate tract could be enclosed.

Good prospects would be those who are passing through trial, whose marriage has broken up, who have grown cold in heart toward God, lonely people who are away from home, those recently bereaved.

Those engaged in children's and youth work should make good use of the power of the pen.

> Only a note, yes only a note,
> To a friend in a distant land.
> The Spirit said 'Write!' but then you had planned
> Some different work, and you thought
> It mattered little, you did not know
> 'Twould have saved a soul from sin and woe,
> You were out of touch with your Lord.

12
Follow-up

This term refers to the instruction and aftercare of the new believer in Christ. It is our responsibility not only to lead people into the new birth, but to nurture them and instruct them in the Christian life. The subject is too large to be treated at length in a book of this small compass. Much excellent literature on this subject is available and should be consulted. However, some brief suggestions are included.

The objective of follow-up is that the new-born child of God may steadily grow in spiritual maturity, and become a functioning member of the church (Eph. 4:13; Col. 1:28). Just as babies are very dependent on parents in early life, so young Christians need the help and guidance of other more mature Christians.

It is not wise to overload such a person with advice, but several things should be emphasised:

1. To be a joyous Christian, he should confess Christ to others at the earliest opportunity, preferably to his own relatives and workmates (Rom. 10:9, 10; Matt. 10:32, 33). The would-be secret disciple will never experience the full joy of the Lord. Explain that if he trusts his newly-found Saviour, he will give him power to testify (Phil. 4:13).

2. Emphasise that Christ is not only his Saviour from sin, but his absolute Lord and Master. Life's questions and problems are to be submitted to Him for His approval and decision. When one becomes a Christian, he takes the crown off his own head and puts it on the head of Jesus. It is no longer Self-control but Christ-control.

3. Urge him to read the Bible every day, preferably first thing in the morning, asking the Holy Spirit to enlighten his mind and make the truth relevant to his daily life. The Bible is to the spiritual life what bread is to the physical life, or

milk to the babe (1 Pet. 2:2). As he reads the Scriptures, God is speaking directly to him. Encourage him to regularly memorise Scripture.

4. Having heard God's voice in the Bible, he should let God hear his voice in prayer. He is invited to pour out his soul and desires in prayer (Matt. 6:6). Encourage the habit of ejaculatory prayer throughout the day as well as the time spent in the secret place.

5. Advise him to begin to work for Christ and endeavour to win others to him. Recently when I was in Los Angeles I met a young man, converted only four months before, who had already led nine of his family circle to Christ.

6. As the whole of the Christian life is inspired and maintained by the Holy Spirit, urge the necessity of being 'filled' or controlled by the Holy Spirit (Eph. 5:18). It is He alone who can keep us walking in fellowship with Christ.

Paul wrote: 'No one can say, "Jesus is Lord", except by the Holy Spirit' (1 Cor. 12:3). That is to say, no one is able to keep Christ on the throne of his life apart from the enabling of the Holy Spirit.

7. Encourage him to join and become a loyal member of an evangelical church. Explain that while one can be a Christian without joining a church, we are exhorted to do so. 'Let us not give up meeting together, as some are in the habit of doing' (Heb. 10:25). From the time of our Lord's ascension, it has been the practice of the church for believers to meet on the first day of the week to worship and praise God, and to hear His Word explained.

The advantages of joining a church are many, especially for a young Christian. There one can find warm fellowship among other Christians and form new friendships. There the Word of God is explained, and instruction given concerning growth in the Christian life. The Apostle Peter likened a young Christian to a newborn baby, and gave this advice: 'Like newborn babies crave pure spiritual milk, so that by it you may grow up in your salvation, now that you have tasted that the Lord is good' (1 Pet. 2:2). The spiritual milk he refers to is the teaching of the Word of God, and the church provides this teaching.

Then too the church can give help and guidance for the development of one's inner life as well as one's outer life of witnessing and service.

No church is perfect but it affords the young Christian fellowship, instruction and guidance that can be gained nowhere else.

Epilogue

It was wartime in Britain. Incendiary bombs were falling all around. A surgeon who had been driving through the streets had to abandon his car and make his way on foot. Suddenly he came on a woman kneeling beside a man who was bleeding profusely. Immediately sensing the situation, he issued an order. 'An immediate operation can save this man's life. Run down to my car and bring my bag of instruments.'

She ran away but returned in five minutes, looking very dejected. 'Doctor, your car has been hit by an incendiary bomb and is completely burnt out.'

'My instruments!' said the surgeon, wringing his hands. 'I could have saved this man's life if only I had my instruments!'

God is looking for instruments whom He can use to bring the Good News to men and women who are 'without God and without hope in the world', but the fact is that so few are available to Him for this purpose.

Have we enough love for souls to lead us to actively seek their salvation? Does the Holy Spirit find a responsive and obedient instrument in us? Shall we not ask God to give us such a revelation of the condition of lost men and women, such a sense of the urgency of their need and our personal responsibility and such an infusion of divine love that we shall travail for souls, and go forth aflame with divine compassion to lead them to Christ?

May it be so, for His sake and for theirs!